STRETCHED

a memoir

MICHELLE CRAY

STRETCHED
Text copyright © 2026
Michelle Cray

This is a true story. Names, identifying characteristics, and details have been changed to protect the privacy of individuals and organizations. Events and dialogues have been recreated from memory and reflect my present recollections of experiences over time.

LCCN 2025927519
ISBN 979-8-218-89312-5

First Edition
1 2 3 4 5 6 7 8 9 10

Editing: Patrick Johns
Cover Design: Getcovers

Acknowledgments

I wish to thank:

My editor, Patrick Johns, for your invaluable advice and hard work. When I hit a wall, you sparked new and genuine ideas that brought this book to life. I cannot thank you enough.

Jennie Girardo, without you, this book wouldn't be here. You cheered me on when I was down. I am beyond grateful for your unwavering support and confidence in me.

Jen Piizzi and Whitney Arons, for your candid and honest feedback, and more importantly, for being great friends. Pat Foglia, for your "non-editor editor" expertise. And the rest of Team V, for being there for me day in and day out.

Daisy Speed, for your support through not only the book writing process, but the unexpected grief I endured toward the end. You were a lifeline.

And of course, Sean, the love of my life. In no other words, I'd be lost without you.

Contents

Introduction

It was the brief moment of sadness between the laughter that revealed a piece of me no one knew. It was the moment few people noticed, unless they too had been through the pain. It was easy for me to put on a happy face, to hide within myself, for fear of shame or embarrassment or what others might think. But with that pain came an unexpected source of strength.

For years, I felt isolated, internalizing the grief I endured throughout my life. The grief that comes with such intimate topics is rarely shared, at least from what I have witnessed, as we have been led to believe our pain is a burden on others. Yet we are the ones who find a sense of freedom in expressing it. This is the sole reason I want to share my story—so that you don't have to feel alone.

This book was written mostly on my phone as I scrambled through the mayhem of my current life. But as I started writing, I couldn't stop. There was something in the process of revealing my stories, acknowledging them, that became cathartic, therapeutic. This is not to say this book didn't take a great deal of courage to publish. It took incredible resolve and commitment to my true objective—to help others. But with that, I felt the intense vulnerability that came along with it, and that to me, was the steepest hurdle to pass.

My story starts when I am five years old and follows my journey through familial hardships and how they affected my upbringing and ensuing relationships into adulthood. It was not until I wrote this book that I truly understood how deeply I was impacted, and even now, I know there is still a lot to learn and digest. I am not a therapist nor licensed in any way for that type of work, so any reflections or insights are my own thoughts and feelings. That is not to say I haven't sought help, and I strongly encourage it, but nothing seemed to strengthen me in the way this book did.

This narrative is based on a true story. If I couldn't rely on memory for some of the events, say because I was too young, I leaned into recollections from family members, who were able to fill in the gaps. Names have been changed to protect the privacy of those who are depicted throughout, and the only real name used is my own. However, I must note that, as with any tale, the perspective is from the storyteller, and that is no different here. I write based on my own journey—and my own feelings in those moments—and that is not to discredit the difficulties others have endured; difficulties that I couldn't quite understand at the time.

For those who know me, this isn't my typical comedic tale. Rather, it dives deep into a fragile psyche as I try to not only understand but validate my experiences. This is probably the first time I have cared to admit that yes, I am damaged, but through it all, I have discovered a profound sense of purpose. I have also accepted that, even though my experiences may not have been ordinary or conventional by any means, finding joy in life is the only way to move past the pain, and one way I have found that is through writing.

By reading my story, you will understand the challenges I faced and the mistakes I made. But with that, you will also see how I handled and sought meaning behind those difficulties. My hope is that this book resonates with you, because you are not alone; there are many others going through the same mental and emotional struggles that come with the challenges of growing up. You can get through it and maybe, just maybe, uncover a truth or two about yourself as well.

—Michelle Cray

For Laura

C h a p t e r 1

The House on Top of The Hill

June 1988

My sister cried faintly, exhausted from weeks of illness that had left her bedridden. My mother sat next to her, frantic. From the hallway outside my parents' bedroom, I peeked my head in through the narrow slit of the door, unsure if I should enter. I cautiously opened it, and as it creaked, my father redirected his attention to me.

"Daddy, what's going on?" I asked timidly as I looked up at him with questioning, innocent eyes.

Dad knelt beside me and placed his hand on my shoulder. "Go to your bedroom, sweetie. Everything will be alright." He responded with compassion, yet I could sense hesitation in his voice.

He stood up and resumed his phone conversation, and as he did so, I embraced his leg, hoping that he would hang up and laugh at my antics. Instead, he tried to remove my grip.

"It's been three weeks, and her fever is still strong," Dad said to whoever was on the phone. Then, he looked down at me, covering the phone with his hand. "Michelle, go to your room. I will be there in a little while." He sounded frustrated. I looked over at my mother who was patting Sam's forehead with a wet washcloth as my two-year-old sister lay shivering under the comforter. I had never seen Mom look so fearful.

"Daddy?" I asked, removing my grasp, but not leaving.

My father ignored me and continued. "If it's bacterial, the antibiotics would have worked. Do you have the results of the blood test yet?" His voice now sounded scared, anxious. He pushed me out of the bedroom, not forcefully, but enough to know I shouldn't go back in.

This was my first memory as a child. I was five years old. To this day, almost forty years later, I remember exactly how I felt, exactly how my sister, my mother, and my father looked, and exactly what I did after I left that bedroom.

Sulking to my room next door, I grabbed my teddy off the floor. "I guess you're my only friend today," I lamented to my stuffed bear. "Sam will come play with us when she's done being sick, right?"

The pastel-pink painted room was adorned with wooden furniture and floral curtains. Situated in the middle of the carpeted floor was a tea set surrounded by the small porcelain dolls that I had arranged in their miniature chairs.

I searched for the picture my sister and I drew on the wall together with colored pencils one afternoon this past spring. My mother was not happy about the new artwork she discovered while putting away our laundry, but she eventually let it slide like she did most things. "Here it is," I said when I found the two stick figures holding hands with big smiles on their faces.

Sam had gotten sick before and she always felt better within a day or two. "Maybe this time, she's just taking a little longer. We'll draw more pictures soon," I said with a naive chuckle. But then, a squirrel scurrying outside the window grabbed my attention. I ran down the stairs and straight out the front door to catch it, but it was long gone.

"Michelle, come back inside," my father shouted from the balcony off the main bedroom. He must have heard me scurry away. "It's about to rain."

"I'm coming, Daddy," I yelled back as I stared at a brightly colored blue-jay perched atop the roof. A thunderclap echoed in the distance.

Our home was what my father called tudor-style. It was covered in white stucco which to me, looked like dried glue, and had these dark brown shutters that flapped in the wind when they came loose. The house stood atop a hill along a tree-lined street in Nutley, a small town in northern New Jersey known for its delis and pizza, robust Italian heritage, and its abundance of parks. To me, the town was quiet and friendly, but I'd always hear Mom rambling on the phone to our neighbor about how my friend Ginnie's mom was sleeping with the gym teacher (though I couldn't understand why going to sleep together was a bad thing), or how the music teacher got fired because he was getting a little too touchy-feely with his grade-school students. Everyone knew everyone, and everyone knew everything.

My parents weren't wealthy, but they were by no means poor

either. My father had a steady job in management for a large engineering firm and dinner was on the table every night. We spent our summers taking expensive vacations and boating in the bay near our four-bedroom beachfront house on Oak Beach, Long Island. Dad's income was sufficient, so my mother stopped working when she gave birth to me. Mom always said she was perfectly happy tending to the house and raising my sister and me. To everyone else, we were the perfect family, tangled up in the American Dream not everyone gets to enjoy.

I walked back into the house, past the long dining table and claw-foot china cabinet to the left and pushed through the swinging doors to the pantry. The stool I brought over from the bathroom was situated below the cabinets next to the bowls filled with dog food and water for our new puppy, Max. I climbed up and grabbed a box of crackers from the cabinet, being careful not to fall back and bang my head like I had done before. I sat at the kitchen table and turned on the small black and white television to the channel airing *I Love Lucy*. It was the one where Lucy works at the chocolate factory, so I happily leaned back into the chair and enjoyed my favorite episode. A few minutes later, the commotion started.

Mom and Dad both rushed down the stairs, my mother moaning something indiscernible. As Mom hurried my sister out the door and into the car, Dad called out, "Michelle, we need to get in the car right away. Put your coat and shoes on and come meet me in the hall."

Normally, I would beg to stay and finish my show, but it was clear to me that I would lose the argument this time. I nervously grabbed my Mary Janes from the floor and as I struggled to put them on, Dad picked me up and carried me down the back stairs to the car. My shoes were dropped into my lap as he strapped me into our 1980 blue Oldsmobile sedan. He barely closed his door before racing in reverse down the winding rocky driveway without saying a word.

"Where are we going, Mommy?" I asked, confused, as we drove down our street, Dad driving faster than usual.

Leaving the house usually meant we were in for a fun day like going to the park or heading to Grandma's, but I knew this was going to be a less enjoyable trip. Neither Mom nor Dad answered my innocent question and remained silent, staring at the road ahead of them.

Heavy rain beat down on the windshield with force. The hot summer storm kept the mid-afternoon sky cloaked in darkness, broken only by the occasional flash of lightning. My father's urgency counteracted the dreary atmosphere surrounding us as he sped through red lights and stop signs, barely avoiding an accident with a small moving truck while he swerved to catch a light. He never drove like this, but I was now too scared to ask any more questions.

Dad finally spoke as he turned into the parking lot filled with cars, "Here it is. Stonewall Hospital."

I looked up at the massive building, in awe of how expansive it was. As I admired the hospital, I was startled by the noise from an ambulance racing by with its lights flashing. Dad parked in a handicap spot, got out of the car, and picked up my sleeping sister from her car seat. He cradled her in his arms as the four of us hurried through the rain to the double doors of the hospital entrance. I followed closely behind my mother as it slowly started to sink in that there was something very wrong with Sam.

The reception area was bustling with medical staff looking hurried and patients looking worn. Dad stood in the center with Sam in his arms, breathless, his hair and clothes soaked.

"Gregory Hanes for Samantha," he shouted to anyone who would listen.

Within seconds, doctors arrived to meet us in the waiting area and took us to a private room where we waited. The room was plain, with only a twin-sized hospital bed and two fabric-lined armchairs filling the space. The fluorescent bulb over the bed flickered. A nurse entered within a few minutes of us being there, took blood from Sam's arm and left quickly without saying much other than "you'll feel a small prick."

"Mommy, I okay?" little Sam asked, now fully awake from her nap, yet still clearly tired as she drooped her head into my mother's lap. She was hesitant, but at the same time seemed to be excited to be surrounded by doctors.

"Sam, do you want to play pretend?" I interrupted enthusiastically, but deep down, feeling like I needed to protect my sister. I didn't know exactly what was happening, but I knew it wasn't good. "I can be the bad guy and you be the superhero trying to catch me!" Sam was weak, but her wide smile and childish giggles answered my question.

"I think that's a great idea," Mom chimed in, looking at me with a smile, as if she was saying "Thank you."

"I'll be the police!" Dad added.

Distracted by the game, it was as if, for a swift moment, we all forgot the reason for our stay. But then, in the aftermath of the storm, the glow from the sun was seen beyond the horizon and the reality of the situation came flooding back. "I want to go home," I said shyly.

"Come here, sweetheart." Dad reached for me and took me into his arms as Mom held Sam on the bed. "It looks like we are going to be staying here for the night. You can sleep here on the chair with me. Everything will be okay."

Then I drifted off, exhausted.

The following morning, a faint light peeked through the blinds and settled onto Sam while I lay peacefully awake in my father's arms. Sam woke up slowly, rubbing her eyes, and looked over at my mother who was sitting close to her. Mom looked like she hadn't slept.

"Is it wake-up time, Mommy?" Sam asked innocently.

"Yes, my little love. The sun is coming up," Mom said quietly.

Dad stirred, stretching slightly, trying to alleviate his stiff back. I looked up at him.

"Hey, Daddy," I said with some sadness. "I didn't give Max any food last night."

"Oh no, Max!" My father must have forgotten about our dog in the rush. "I'll call Harry later this morning to walk and feed him. He'll be okay, sweetie." Our neighbor was a good friend of Mom and Dad's, willing to help when needed.

A little while later, Doctor Paginta entered the room. He was short and thin, organized with a clipboard in hand and oversized glasses on his face. He looked almost melancholy though and Mom stared at his somber demeanor, while I noticed her sudden frown and the tears filling her eyes. Then, for some reason, I suddenly felt sad too.

"Hello, Mr. and Mrs. Hanes. It is nice to see you again," Doctor Paginta said solemnly.

My father also noticed the look on the doctor's face. "Oh no, no please don't say it," my father cried.

"We need to transport Samantha to the Newark Children's Hospital oncology ward right away. Your daughter has Acute Lymphocytic Leukemia."

Chapter 2
Nothing is Certain

Acute Lymphocytic Leukemia? I thought. As a young child, I had no idea what it meant, but I knew by the tone in everyone's voice, it was not good. It was not until many years later that I fully understood and was told exactly what happened in the days leading up to Sam's hospitalization.

A few weeks prior, Sam had fallen ill with a high fever. My parents, assuming it was most likely a seasonal illness most kids get at her age, gave her some over-the-counter medicine and told her to rest. It was when the fever remained high despite the medication that their concern mounted. Sam was brought to her local pediatrician who was quick to attribute it to a staph infection she had weeks prior.

But the fever lingered and another week passed with no change in Sam's condition. At that point, she was referred to a different physician at one of the nearby hospitals, Stonewall, who collaborated with the head of the pediatrics unit. They echoed her pediatrician's diagnosis, appearing to dismiss the issue, and attributed it to an illness related to the infection. They ordered more fever-reducing medicine to keep her comfortable. Still, Sam showed no signs of improvement.

Frustrated, my father requested a fresh review of her case and Doctor Paginta took over. After reviewing Sam's records, he rejected the earlier assessments almost immediately and relayed his suspicion of cancer to my father over the phone. To confirm the diagnosis, he ordered additional blood tests to be taken right away, and that is when we rushed Sam to Stonewall Hospital.

My mother and father sat bleary-eyed on the edge of Sam's bed, listless. We were all exhausted, and although the doctor just confirmed that Sam had cancer, my parents seemed surprisingly calm. I think they were in shock though.

"Okay, um, can you tell us more?" my mother asked, her voice shaky. "What does this mean for our daughter?"

Doctor Paginta continued in a soothing, calm voice. "We are unable to give you much information here without running more tests. The children's hospital specializes in cancer treatment and will be able to help you further. I'm sorry."

"No, please. You must tell us more," Mom pleaded. "You can't say my daughter has cancer and then walk away."

"Mommy, what's cancer?" I asked but was quickly ignored.

"I agree with my wife," Dad said. "What else can you tell us?"

"I am sorry as I'm sure this is difficult to process. There are a few options but since I'm not an expert in this area, I think it's best you speak with Doctor Gerard, the pediatric cancer specialist," Doctor Paginta said. He then left the room to prepare the discharge papers.

My mother looked at my father, her eyes welled with tears. I looked at her, wanting to give her a hug, but also afraid that I would be rejected again. I also felt the urge to cry but stopped myself knowing it wouldn't make a difference.

"Help me, Greg," she pleaded.

"Okay, he said she has cancer, but did you see him? He didn't seem too concerned, right? It sounds like she will be okay." Dad always offered a sense of practicality, a way to calm the room in highly emotional moments. This time though, it seemed like he was trying to convince himself too. "Maybe there is a new medicine, or treatment we don't know about."

"I hope you're…"

Mom was interrupted by a nurse we didn't recognize, who walked in quite unexpectedly. None of us even realized she was in the room until she started to speak in a slow, somber tone. "I want to offer my condolences," she said as we all looked in her direction. "I will pray deeply for your family. No little girl deserves this. No family deserves this." She bowed her head and left the room.

It was at this moment, and the fact that this nurse came in solely to offer her prayers, that the severity of the situation seemed to hit both my parents. My mother started wailing, and my father sat stunned. Sam and I were on the bed, cuddled together. I was doing my best to keep Sam occupied with a children's book because even though I wasn't crying like Mom and Dad, I knew she shouldn't hear any of this.

Shortly after being discharged, we drove Sam straight to Newark Children's Hospital, but this time, the ride was quiet. There was no rain beating down on the windshield, no screeching of the tires as my father made the turns. Just silence.

Dad drove much more slowly too, as he was very clearly disturbed by the information he was given, and I could see Mom's hands clenched into his as they lay on the center console.

The Children's Hospital was situated in the city of Newark, surrounded by run-down buildings and storefronts, all decorated in graffiti. People rushed about the sidewalks, trying to get to work or wherever else they needed to go. I admired the hospital, the same way I did the last, but this time, I felt uneasy.

When we walked in through the double doors of the hospital, we were escorted to a room in the pediatric oncology ward. It was dull like the first, but larger and filled with two twin beds separated by a single curtain, two sets of oversized chairs, a small television, and medical equipment. The walls were white, but a few close family members who were told of the situation had flowers and cards delivered to brighten up the space. My father requested a cot for me when he was told by the staff that we would be at the hospital for at least a few weeks.

Doctor Gerard walked into the room with a composed expression and introduced himself. He was an older gentleman, tall and thin, and straightforward. If there was something that needed to be said, he said it. Yet below his no-nonsense exterior, he exhibited a quiet warmth, one that could calm a room with a simple glance. I looked at him with a smile because even though I didn't love doctors or hospitals, I felt oddly comfortable around him.

"I'm Doctor Gerard and will be taking over for Sam's treatment. How are you, Sam?" he asked, turning toward my sister, his face bright.

"Tired," Sam said. Mom and Dad looked concerned.

"That's okay. We'll get this bed comfy for you with some more blankets. I'll tell you what. Do you think you can keep an eye on my favorite walrus?" Doctor Gerard held up a plush toy he pulled from behind his back and handed it to Sam. "Her name is Penny."

"Yes! Hi, Penny!" Sam said happily as I ran over to her to see the new plush.

"Mr. and Mrs. Hanes," Doctor Gerard said, re-directing his attention to my parents. "Do you mind if we speak over by the door for a moment?"

"Sure. Girls, please stay here," my father told us. I didn't move an inch knowing full well by now that I was not invited. Sam was busy with her new distraction.

The door was slightly ajar, and from Sam's bed, I could hear the steady beeps from the heart monitors in each of the neighboring rooms. Though I wasn't standing next to my parents, I could hear everything as Doctor Gerard took on a more serious tone. "Your daughter has acute lymphocytic leukemia. We will begin the first stage of treatment right away and I expect it to last about one month. Sam will remain in the hospital the entire time. Right now, we need to focus on destroying the cancer cells in the blood and bone marrow and get her fever under control."

"How is that done?" my father asked.

Doctor Gerard paused. "Through chemotherapy that will be administered here at the hospital. I want you to understand, this won't be easy. The treatment involves painful procedures, but she's a young girl and she's strong. I will be here every step of the way as I'm sure both of you will too."

"Of course," my father said.

"You mentioned painful procedures," my mother said. "What do you mean?" Even I was curious about what the doctor meant by that.

"The chemotherapy will tire her out and make her feel unwell, often nauseous, unfortunately," Doctor Gerard said.

"We will be right next to her during it all," my mother said.

"But that's not it," the doctor said. Just then, Sam dropped the stuffed animal, and I jumped off the bed to grab it, still listening in. The doctor continued. "We will need to perform spinal taps at different intervals throughout her treatment, and they may cause a bit of discomfort. We can give her some pain relievers to help, but it won't be much."

"A spinal tap? What exactly is done during a spinal tap?" my father asked, his voice sounding heavy.

"We need to know if the cancer spreads. A needle will be injected into her lower back to withdraw fluid. The process from start to finish will last about fifteen minutes."

My father spoke softly now. "Oh my, that sounds terrible. Is there anything we can do to make her feel more comfortable?"

"Just be there with her. We will get through this," Doctor Gerard said. "I will come back later today and give you a more detailed explanation of how we intend to proceed, but for now, it is imperative that we begin chemotherapy immediately. Do you have any other questions for me at this time?"

"One more," my father said. I saw him squeeze my mother's hand. "What are...what are the chances?"

The doctor responded, "Like I said, she is young and she is strong. I will run some more tests, and I should have a better answer for you over the next few days."

"Thank you," my father said. He and my mother turned around with their heads down. They walked back to the bed to give us both a hug.

Minutes later, nurses came into the room to administer the chemotherapy I.V., which was inserted into a vein in Sam's arm. Once it was in, she tried to wriggle it free, complaining that the spot itched but she eventually adjusted to the feel of it.

It was kept in position for a few days, at which time, Sam was prepped for her first spinal tap. Two nurses entered along with the doctor, and my father was asked to hold Sam in his lap with his arms wrapped tightly around her body. The doctor then began the process of inserting the needle into her tiny back, flexing her spine to ensure it didn't hit the bone. A moment later, Sam screamed in a way that crumbled my heart.

~

In the days that followed, my parents immersed themselves in learning about leukemia. The hospital staff supplied books and materials brimming with medical information, much of it complex and difficult to grasp. Yet, from the multitude of pages of clinical jargon, one sobering fact stood out, one that the doctor side-stepped a few days earlier. I overheard my parents say the five-year survival rate for this type of leukemia was a mere sixty-five percent.

Time slowed, almost crawled. Every day, every hour, every minute, we did not know if Sam would succumb to the thirty-five percent, if I would ever be able to play with my sister again. My heart sunk at the thought.

It was a long, distressing week, but Sam's condition started to improve and her temperature fell to a normal level. Sam was tired, her hair started to thin, and her cheeks were puffy from the steroids she was given to boost her immune system, but our hopes were starting to look up.

"Hi honey, how are you feeling?" Mom asked as Sam struggled to open her eyes from her afternoon nap.

"Mom, why is that machine so loud?" I interrupted as the heart monitor started beeping.

Mom picked Sam up and yelled out for a nurse. One rushed in and paged Doctor Gerard, who ordered an immediate blood test as Sam lay limp in my mother's arm. That was the thing I learned about leukemia—stability could turn to urgency at any moment.

We all anxiously awaited the test results as Sam slept. Every second passed with the hope that the doctor would come back with news on how to proceed, but it wasn't until two hours later that he returned.

The doctor spoke calmly, yet quickly. "Sam's red blood cell count has dropped significantly. She needs to have a blood transfusion immediately."

I couldn't understand. Sam had been doing so well. "Why is this happening?" My mother asked the question I was thinking.

"Mrs. Hanes, I'm sorry, we need to get her prepped. I promise you, I'll explain when I have a moment."

My mother turned to my father with a look of shocked pain. "Greg, I can't handle this. My baby. My heart." She clutched her chest.

"Mommy, is Sam okay?" I asked.

At that moment, when my parents didn't look away or brush aside my question, I knew they were finally going to explain the situation, to confirm my fears. "Michelle, Sam is very, very sick," Mom told me. She was speaking low and calmly, but on the brink of tears.

"Like when I was sneezing really badly last week?" I asked timidly. I knew it was more significant than that, but I didn't quite know the full extent of it, nor how to tell them what I was thinking.

Dad spoke now. "It's a little more than that. Sam has what we call cancer. It's like a lot of bad germs that we need to get rid of and unfortunately it won't be easy." I could only imagine how hard it was for my father to communicate this to a five-year-old.

"Well, we can just give her medicine, right?" I asked. My innocence made them smile.

"Oh sweetie. We will," Mom said. "The doctors are going to work very hard to try and cure her. That's why we are staying here—so they can help her."

Her words calmed my nerves. "Okay. I just want Sam better, Mommy," I said. That is really all I wanted.

"We do too."

For the next few hours while Sam received the transfusion in her bed, Mom paced the room nervously, as Dad made calls to family members. I sat on my cot, making bracelets with the beads Dad bought from the gift shop, until I nodded off. When I woke up, the doctor had just returned.

"Sam is responding well," he said.

"Oh, thank God," Mom sighed.

"She has what we call chemotherapy-induced anemia," the doctor explained. "It's common and may seem scary, but the transfusion is relatively straightforward and should help."

Over the next day, Sam's low red blood cell counts improved, but even though things were looking better, I remained on edge. It was clear that even though my sister was looking healthier, it didn't mean she wasn't very seriously ill.

~

Two full weeks had passed since Sam was admitted to Newark Children's Hospital. Sam slept soundly in her bed while I quietly skimmed through a few children's books brought from home. The initial threat to Sam's health seemed to subside little by little each day and though I was getting used to our new environment, I was longing to get back home to Max and everything else in my life.

My parents sat in the nearby chairs, Dad reading the newspaper, Mom a book. Not long after Sam was admitted, Mikey, a young boy who was not much older than Sam and battling a similar form of cancer, was placed in the room with us. Donna sat next to her son, holding his hand as he slept peacefully, and Charles, his father, had just returned from speaking with the doctor.

Despite having only recently met, my parents formed a close relationship with Charles and Donna, drawn together by the unspoken bond of fear, hope, and love for their children. Neither family was prepared for the reality that had suddenly fallen upon them and neither had any idea what the future held. So, we all prayed. We prayed hard, hoping the worst would not befall either of us because we all knew everything could change in a split second.

My father put his book down and glanced at Sam, who was sleeping peacefully. Then he looked over at Donna. "I'm so scared. She's only two years old. All I want to do is keep her happy and I don't know how to do that when she's here in this dreadful place," he agonized.

"Daddy, what do you mean?" I interrupted.

"Oh, sweetie, Sam is still sick but she's going to be okay. Please go back to reading your books."

I felt the sting yet again of trying to understand but instead, getting cast aside. I now knew that what Sam had was serious, but it also seemed like she was getting better. *Why did my father still seem so dismal?* I went back to looking at the pictures in my book but found that I was concentrating more on the conversation in the room than on the Berenstain Bears.

"Our Mikey is as happy as he can be with us here. All you can do is be there for her," Donna reassured him. "Just be her dad." She was a quiet young woman, shy but seemingly open with my parents.

"Donna, how can you stay so calm?" Mom asked. "I feel like I want to explode at any given moment. I've been crying for days, and it feels like this will never end."

"Oh, don't be confused. I feel like a volcano about to erupt," Donna said. "I just don't know what good that will do for any of us right now."

"We need to stay strong for our kids," Dad added. "If we don't, she won't—" He teared up and grabbed my mother's hand.

"Oh, thank goodness she's sleeping right now," he said, and I could see the sympathetic looks on everyone's faces.

It felt like an instant, but one short week later, Mikey lost his fight with leukemia, and his little body was slowly unhooked from the medical machines and taken away. He was stolen from this world and all it left was heartache and pain, a sadness that could never be cured. And just like that, Charles and Donna were never seen at the children's hospital again.

Sam, confused about her now missing friend, asked, "Mommy, where's Mikey?"

I knew. I didn't say a word, but I knew. And suddenly, it hit me—nothing was certain. I walked over and sat close to Sam with my arms around her as Mom continued speaking.

"Oh, my little sweetheart. Mikey had to go. Mikey said he loves you and will miss you very much." Mom's voice was so tense that I thought she was going to scream.

And then she did.

Mom screamed so loudly, the hospital floor echoed with her high-pitched shriek. Sam sat motionless, confused, and I—well, I understood. Medical staff came running in to find my mother on the floor sobbing. My father, who had been grabbing a snack down at the cafe had just returned. As he realized what had happened, he dropped the small bag of food all over the floor and ran over to console her. My mother was slowly breaking crack by small crack.

Chapter 3

The Space Between Moods

July 1988

Sam's condition improved over the next three weeks. Dad started going back to work and I spent some time at Aunt Francine's with my cousins who were also around my age. Every night though, Dad and I both returned to Mom and Sam in the hospital for a few hours until one of them would take me home so I could sleep in my own bed.

As much as I missed home, the house felt empty without my sister. Sam and I shared a room before she got sick and I just wanted her in her bed and me in mine, giggling at silly things before we both drifted off to sleep. But now that she wasn't there, I felt uncomfortable, almost scared to be alone.

One night though, I was so tired that I fell asleep as soon as my head hit the pillow. I had a dream that Sam wasn't sick anymore. Instead, we were running together under a rainbow that spread out over our backyard, sparkling in the sunshine. We were kids, happy to be back together, without a care in the world.

The next morning, when I woke up, I immediately felt the sadness taking over. Dad helped me get dressed and we returned to the hospital after picking up some doughnuts along the way to cheer me up. Sam sat comfortably in her hospital bed, stacking blocks, as Sesame Street played on the small television. Mom grabbed a wooden block from the bed and handed it to Sam who placed it on the top of her tower. It fell to the floor and crashed.

"I want to go home!" Sam cried loudly, inconsolable. Mom walked over to comfort her and somehow remained composed as Sam screamed.

"We should be going home soon. I promise," Mom told her, though I could tell she was just as antsy waiting for more news. Doctors and nurses were in and out of our room constantly but none who could give us the go-ahead to move forward. It was only when Doctor Gerard walked into the room smiling a few hours later that all our eyes gleamed with hope.

"I'm very happy to report, we can further Sam's treatment," he relayed. "She is now out of the induction phase and will no longer need heavy chemotherapy."

"Oh, thank you, thank you!" Mom cried cheerfully. This made me laugh out loud, something I hadn't done in weeks.

"Thank you so much, Doctor Gerard. What does this mean for phase two?" my father asked, showing his appreciation. I could tell he was holding back from displaying too much excitement though.

"Consolidation involves more chemotherapy, though less intense and can be given in pill form at home, meaning you will be released today. There will be a rather complex schedule of when the medicine should be taken, and it will change as her condition changes. But she made it through the first stage, and I want you to focus on that right now," Doctor Gerard explained. "She's doing great."

"This is good news," Dad said.

Mom looked at us and gleamed with excitement, "We can go home today girls!"

Sam and I yelled with joy and gave each other a hug. We would finally be able to go home as a family once again.

The house on top of the hill was quiet when we returned, and we were all able to sleep in our own beds. Dad tucked each of us in and as he did every evening, read a story, and kissed us goodnight.

~

Over the next few weeks, our lives started to return to normal. They were filled with doctor's appointments, blood draws, and spinal taps, but it was clear Sam was responding very well to treatment and would soon be cleared to enter the final phase of care. Up until this point, Mom had been with Sam most of the time, so I was surprised when she asked Dad if she could spend some quality time with me while he drove Sam to the hospital for her next spinal tap, which still had to be done every two to three weeks. Dad agreed.

I was excited to hang out with Mom and ran to the playroom to grab some toys for us to play with. As I was doing so, I heard an unexpected wail from the kitchen. I quickly ran over to see that Dad was consoling Sam.

"Daddy, I'll be good! Please don't do this anymore. I promise I'll be good!" Sam screamed, begging my father not to take her to the next appointment. She blamed herself for the suffering. I stared in disbelief, wondering how she could even think that.

"Sweetheart, this is not your fault. You did absolutely nothing wrong," Dad said, pausing to take a deep breath and compose himself.

"You know what, Sam?" I interrupted. "I'll have a surprise for you when you get home!"

"Surprise? For me?" Sam's eyes immediately lit up and just like that, she forgot where she was headed.

"Yes! Just for you. For being the best sister in the whole world!" I pressed on, trying my best to keep her mind occupied.

"Oh boy!" Sam said, and she walked out the back door with a smile on her face.

On the way back to the playroom, I noticed Mom hadn't moved from the couch even though Sam was crying loudly.

"Mommy, can you play with me?" I asked.

"Oh, uh, hey, I have to take care of a few things right now. Here, let me grab you some crayons and colored paper so you can draw," she said. "I think I overheard you saying you wanted to give Sam a surprise when she got home?"

"Yes!"

I sat down at the dining room table with my art supplies and began drawing on pink-colored paper. Mom trudged up the stairs and out of my view. I was almost finished with my card when I started to worry that I hadn't seen her in twenty minutes and decided to find out what she was doing. I skipped up the stairs, happy to have something ready for Sam, and opened the door to her bedroom. There, my mother lay fast asleep.

"Mommy?" I tried to wake her up, knowing that I wasn't supposed to be left alone.

She grunted and rolled over to her side. I wasn't scared, just a little confused, but figured she was very tired. I picked up the blanket sprawled across the foot of the bed and placed it over her. I walked back downstairs to add some final touches to the card and cleaned up the crayons. Then, I sat on the couch and turned on the television to my favorite show.

An hour later, Dad carried Sam through the front door right up to me on the couch. I immediately gave her a hug. "Sam! I made you something!" I exclaimed, running over to the dining room table to grab her card. On the front in large letters were the words, "I love you!" written with purple crayon. Inside were two stick figures, much like the ones on the wall of my room, but these had a large rainbow drawn over them. "This is our rainbow. Only we can slide down it!"

"I love you!" Sam said. She took the card and sat on the floor admiring the picture. She still looked down from her spinal tap, but her mood seemed to have lifted from my simple gesture. "Mommy, look!" Sam said excitedly.

My mother plodded down the stairs, rubbing her eyes—she must have just woken up from her nap. I had noticed that recently, Mom's mood was shifting, and it was happening rather suddenly.

"Have you been upstairs this whole time?" Dad asked her, concerned.

"Michelle's fine, darling," she snapped sarcastically. "She's been watching Sesame Street."

"I love Big Bird, Daddy!" I added.

"You told me you wanted to spend quality time with her. You can't just leave her all day by herself," Dad said angrily.

"We had a tea party with her dolls before I took a very quick nap," Mom lied. "Calm down."

"No, we…" I started to say.

"It was so much fun! Right, Michelle?" Mom interrupted.

I nodded, not knowing what else to say.

Dad was still angry. "You know exactly how my parents treated me when I was a child and I will not let that happen to our girls."

"Oh, get over it," Mom growled back, provoked. She stomped into the kitchen like a toddler who was refused a candy bar. Sam and I stood still, not saying a word. We were frightened.

Dad knelt to our level. "Hey kids. It'll be okay. Mommy's just going through a rough patch, but I'm sure she will be out to play with you later today!"

"Okay, Daddy," I said. Then I took Sam's hand in mine and led her off to the playroom. I opened the trunk of costumes my mother had prepared for us and called out to Max who came running over. Minutes later, our dog was wearing a princess dress, a hat…and a frown.

Although Sam's health continued to improve for the next month and the doctors officially declared she had entered the final stage of treatment called maintenance, Mom had sunk into a deep depression. Dad had been working later hours and took a job as a night-school teacher to help cover the medical bills and to keep the family's health insurance secure, but his constant absence had taken a toll on the family dynamic. I had recently started kindergarten so in addition to cleaning, laundry, bathing, preparing meals, and getting me ready for school, Mom was now responsible for more significant obligations, including administering Sam's medication at the correct time of day, driving to and from bi-weekly doctor appointments, and keeping me away from Sam when I was sick because even a slight cold could warrant a trip to the hospital.

Alongside the stress of taking care of us and tending to the house, my mother always seemed sad and anxious, and I could only imagine if she constantly wondered if the cancer flowing inside Sam would take her. It was as if the grief was controlling her and she began to withdraw.

It was a Wednesday night, and I knew what that meant. "Daddy's working late again?" I sighed to Mom at the dinner table.

"Yes, your father said he would be home earlier than usual tonight though," she reassured me. "Dinner's ready."

"What are we having?" I knew I would be disappointed. The only answer I ever wanted to hear was "pizza", or "lasagna" if I was lucky.

"Chicken cutlets."

"Yay!" Sam shouted excitedly. She loved chicken cutlets.

"Mom, I hate chicken cutlets," I whined.

"It's the dinner I made, and you will eat it, or you will eat nothing. I don't care," Mom said apathetically. I was startled by her response. I remained quiet and Mom's tone changed as she realized she may have been too harsh. "I'll put *I Love Lucy* on the television," she said in a calmer voice.

"Fine," I responded, defeated.

Max began yapping loudly. Sam and I shouted in excitement as Dad entered through the back door into our muted 1980's-style kitchen. He was soaking wet as he walked from the bus stop at the end of the street to the house.

"I forgot my damn umbrella," he complained. "Hi girls!" he said, walking over to the dinner table and plopping in his seat, exhausted.

"Daddy! I made a butterfly at..." I started speaking but was interrupted by Mom.

"You're dripping. Please change," Mom said tersely.

"I want to see the girls," Dad said, resisting. "I'll go change in a minute."

"Dinner is ready now. I'm not waiting," Mom snapped more strongly this time.

"I'll be right back girls." My father removed his shoes and hurried upstairs to change. Returning in dry clothes, he resumed his seat at the table as Mom served dinner.

"Sam's medication protocol changed again today. I don't know if I can keep up with this," Mom sighed, scooping mashed potatoes onto our plates.

"We should talk about this later, don't you think?" Dad questioned her as he looked directly at us.

Then, Mom slammed the pot down on the table and without saying a word, stomped through the kitchen doors and into the living room. The roaring shout from the other side of the house caused Dad to jump up abruptly and run, as we followed closely behind. Mom grabbed a decorative plate from the fireplace mantle and threw it at the wall. Glass shattered everywhere.

"Girls, you stay there," Dad ordered, and like statues, we froze, utterly frightened.

Mom started to scream, shaking. "I am so sick of being the one responsible for everything in this damn house! You are never around! I'm losing it!"

Dad gently approached her and offered a hug. "I know this is hard," he said calmly, but Mom pushed him off.

"You know this is hard? Michelle was sick with strep last week. Who had to keep her away from Sam so she wouldn't end up in the hospital again? Who do you think makes sure they are both fed, bathed, and dressed? Who keeps the nonstop pile of dishes clean? All I want is a damn dishwasher, Greg!" Mom cried and dropped to the floor.

Dad tried to console her as we looked on from the corner of the room. "I'm sorry. I know this isn't easy on you. I'll try to help more," he promised. "Please take a breath. The kids are right over there."

Mom's face softened as she looked at us. She took a moment and extended her arm, beckoning us as we inched toward her. Shards of broken glass were still spread over the carpet on the other side of the room. We sat in her lap and looked up at her with wide, uncertain eyes as Mom began to weep uncontrollably, holding us tightly.

"Mommy, are you sad?" I asked.

"I'm a little sad, yes," she replied, wiping tears from her cheeks.

"It's okay to be sad," I offered.

Sam kissed her on the cheek. "Mommy all better," she said in her sweet toddler voice. A fragile smile broke through Mom's tears and Dad pulled the family together in a tight embrace, trying his best to mend the rift that was growing deeper by the day.

Chapter 4

A Life Imagined

October 1977

Mom and Dad's paths crossed when they were in their early twenties. Mom was twenty-three, two years younger than my father when they met in the late 1970s. His six-foot-two thin but muscular stature towered over my mother, who stood at a shorter five-foot-four inches. The beginning of their love story was simple, but one that changed the course of their lives forever.

My father, Greg, was a handsome man with thick curly black hair, dark eyes, and light German skin. He grew up in Nutley, New Jersey in a two-story colonial with his sister, Patricia, who was ten years his senior. Dad and Patricia did not have a typical sibling relationship due to their wide age gap, but they were supportive of each other.

Dad's father passed away when I was very young, and I only have vague recollections of him. He was a baker, and a more private, simple man, keeping to himself most of the time. Immersed in his work, he had to be out of the house by three in the morning to prepare for the day ahead and would return well after my father and his sister were put to bed for the night. My grandfather's determination, as well as his wife's success, bode well for the family financially though and money was never hard to come by.

When I was a child, I loved visiting Grandma, my father's mother. She was a plump woman, with shiny gray hair, a twinkle in her eye, and a sense of humor only few people understood—me being one of them. Before I was born, Grandma was a well-known vocalist, performing on the grand stages of Radio City or Carnegie Hall, and when she retired years later, she continued her passion of art by teaching voice lessons in their home. She taught until I was old enough to remember, and I would watch in awe at her ability to play piano with such ease, her beautiful voice filling the room.

It came as a surprise to me when I found out years later that my father had a strained relationship with her growing up. He recalled to me with a pained expression that she was often apathetic toward him, at times leaving him alone to entertain himself while she tended to her own needs. As a child, he felt alone, neglected.

With unrequited love from his parents, my father chose to focus on his studies and performed well in school. He graduated from a private college with a bachelor's degree in business administration and started his career in management at Penter Corporation, the same place my mother worked as a secretary. I was told the story of how they met only recently.

A quick glance from my father as he walked past the document library made him pause. He watched the young woman awkwardly trying to fix the heel of her kitten-toe sandal. My mother looked plain in her tan pantsuit, yet so radiant, and her clumsiness made him chuckle. Hesitantly, he stepped into the room and knelt beside her on the floor.

My father was shy but took advantage of the opportunity. "Do you, uh, do you need help with that?" he asked.

Mom was taken aback. "Oh! I didn't see you there!" she exclaimed. When she looked up, their eyes met and she felt her cheeks flush. "Thank you," she said. "That's very sweet of you."

"My name's Greg," he said. "I don't know too much about shoes, but I can try my best. Let me see."

My mother laughed and handed my father her shoe, and as she did, her hand lightly grazed his.

"I'm sorry, I didn't catch your name," my father apologized, looking directly into her eyes.

"Janet," she replied. "And don't worry. I clearly don't know much about shoes either."

He smiled.

My mother was raised in Jersey City, New Jersey in a small two-family house. An Italian-German beauty with long wavy dark hair, she had deep brown eyes, a heart-shaped face, and smooth fair skin. The second youngest of six children, three boys and three girls, she and her brother, Larry, were the babies of the family, and treated that way, often the unsuspecting subjects in a game of dress-up. Her older sisters, Gail and Francine, were eight and six years older, respectively, and though my mother was much younger, they shared a bond that lasted well into adulthood. The three brothers, George, John, and Larry were close with their sisters, but their affection was more protective than playful. The family tie was strong.

My mother's father was the breadwinner of the household and owned a family photography business, one that he started with two of his brothers. He was an honest businessman and industrious; sixteen-hour shifts were a regular occurrence. His daily routine involved gathering film from local convenience stores, developing them in his studio at home and returning the pictures for payment. However, when the photography industry boomed in the 1950s and Kodak surged in popularity, many smaller, family-owned businesses fell by the wayside. My grandfather went from having a steady income to days when money was scarce, sometimes bringing home no more than a few pennies for his hard work. At one point, as his business struggled, he purchased a peanut-roasting machine and started delivering nuts to supplement his income, a testament to how desperate he was to provide for his family. They made do with what they had though, evidenced only by the fact that my grandmother, "Nanny" as we called her, always had food on the table.

Nanny, from what I remember, was a good woman. She was short and thin and had these beautiful loose red curls that sat on top of her head, almost like those of Lucille Ball. I was told Nanny was nurturing and selfless when my mother was growing up, but I remember her as strict, probably because she rarely let me get away with my antics the way Mom did.

My mother studied hard and did well in high school. She formed close friendships with a few other girls but was not overly popular and more of a loner, often keeping to herself. When she graduated high school, she attended a small college in Jersey City, which at the time was an accomplishment for most women. However, she had to drop out halfway through due to the family's financial constraints and had no choice but to get a job. At the time, women studied to work in one of three professional fields: teaching, secretarial, or nursing. I can't count how many times Mom told me she wanted to be a nurse.

When my father and mother first met, it was young love, the type seen in romantic dramas or romance novels. Their melodic laughter was entangled with intense jealousy, but the type that kept their fierce spark alive. My mother would fall deeply into my father's arms at the end of the day as if he were the solution to all the world's problems. She loved him and he her, and it seemed as if nothing could get in their way.

On a rainy day in 1979, they lay in bed together, my mother still sleeping, stirring slightly as she began to wake. My father reached into the bedside table for a small box, and sat there, his heart beating wildly as my mother awakened. He knew her answer, but there was still something remarkable about the moment. They shared their vows in the summer of 1980 during a large Catholic ceremony at a church in the town where my father had been raised.

A year later, my parents purchased his family-owned house across town for full market price. This house, the one where Sam and I were raised, was built in 1914 by Dad's grandfather. He lived there with my great-grandmother for almost sixty years before passing away suddenly from a heart attack. My great-grandmother lived there for several more years before she had a stroke and had to be moved into my grandmother's house to be cared for. At that point, the old house remained empty for two years until 1981 when my parents moved in.

Although the dark woodwork and mahogany built-in furniture remained original to the house, the electrical, plumbing, appliances, walls, and ceilings all needed updating or repair. Despite the complete home renovation required, it was the perfect house to raise a family. Each room in the house was surrounded by four walls except for the dining room, which opened to the entry and flowed into the living room. Stairs near the front door led to the second floor, which had a full bathroom and three large bedrooms—one painted light purple, which served as a nursery when Sam and I were babies. There was an eat-in kitchen, a large backyard, and the sunroom near the front made the perfect playroom. The balcony overlooking the front yard was unique to the neighborhood and my favorite feature.

My mother and father undertook the extensive renovation and in November 1982, while the electrical work was still being completed, my mother went into labor. They rushed to Stonewall Hospital and a day later, I was born.

Chapter 5

Speechless

March 1989

A few months had passed since Mom's emotional outburst, but her depression kept sinking deeper, affecting every aspect of our lives—from getting us dressed in the morning to cooking dinner at night. Mom had a hard time waking up at dawn, so Dad made sure Sam received her medication first thing in the morning before he left for work. And although Sam was relatively stable and acting more like a toddler each day, she was worn out from chemotherapy and needed comfort. Dad was still working late hours at the office and kept his job as a teacher, and although he had taken on slightly more responsibility in the home, he was rarely around.

"Hey, Mommy! I'm home," I shouted as I walked through the front door after a friend's mom dropped me off from school one day. I was now six years old and Sam had just turned three. My mood quickly changed to wonder when I saw my mother. "What are you doing?" I asked. She was wiping down the windowsills, but not in the typical manner—she was so frantic, it reminded me of one of those silly cartoons I'd watch.

"Cleaning!" Mom exclaimed. "I have an idea!" She was over-excited, skipping back and forth between the living room and the dining room.

"Where's Sam?" I asked, my wonderment turning to concern.

"Who? Oh, Sam. She's right over there!" Mom's eyes were wide with elation. She pointed at Sam who was sitting on the couch smiling at us. "Here, come with me!"

Mom led us into the kitchen as we followed happily behind. Then she, quite unexpectedly, took a large basin from the sink and flipped it, pouring water all over the tan-colored vinyl floor.

"Mom, what are you doing?!" I asked, entertained.

"Watch this!" Mom then took the liquid soap bottle from the cabinet under the sink, turned it over, and squeezed it onto the floor. Mountains of bubbles started to form as she swished around the mixture and Sam and I laughed wholeheartedly. Mom laughed hysterically, watching me slip-slide across the floor, and Sam climbed up into the large sink and began to fling bubbles onto the ceiling. I hadn't seen Sam this happy since before she got sick.

About twenty minutes later, Dad walked through the front door. "I'm home!" he shouted happily unaware of what was happening as he made his way to the small commotion in the kitchen. "I left work early to surprise you." The moment he spotted the bubbly chaos, he stopped, his expression shifting instantly to one of concern. "What is going on? Janet, please get over here!"

"Oh Greg, you're such a downer," Mom sighed. "We are having fun."

"Girls, get a towel and go sit in the other room. I need to talk to your mom for a minute," Dad said sternly.

"But Dad," I whined.

"Just do it."

I knew never to argue with my father when he was angry. Whenever I would talk back or use my "sassy" voice as he'd like to call it, he would chase after me with his belt. He never actually hit me with it, but I was too scared to find out if the next time would be different. I instead grabbed two towels from the bathroom and sat down next to Sam in one of the high-back chairs in the dining room, waiting for our parents to return. We could hear every word of their conversation.

Mom fought back, still frenzied. "We were just having a little fun. The girls were the happiest I've seen them in months."

"Maybe, but what message are we sending to the girls if we say playing slip and slide in the kitchen is okay?" Dad questioned.

"Fine, whatever." Mom abruptly ended whatever discussion they were having. "Girls! Come back! We'll order pizza for dinner." We cheered back in excitement.

Mom's manic episode didn't subside for another few days, at which time, she fell yet again into sadness. I could tell something was very wrong, but there was nothing Mom could do, nor anything Dad could say, that would change her sudden and drastic emotional fluctuations. Dad became not only increasingly worried but also desperate to figure out what was going on. He turned to Nanny for some type of explanation.

"Hi, Marie. It's Greg. Do you have a minute?" Dad had called Mom's mother while Mom was out with Sam. I was sitting on the floor watching some cartoon on the television that barely kept my attention.

I could only hear muffled words from Nanny on the other end, something about dinner and my grandfather, but after a few moments, Dad continued in a low voice.

"Janet's been, well her mood has been, off," my father said. "She's having episodes, explosive ones. I had been chalking it up to what we have been going through with Sam, but I think this is something different. There are many times when she doesn't make sense at all. Do you know what could be going on?"

As Nanny spoke, Dad paused and I waited.

"What kind of episodes did your husband have?" my father asked when she was done speaking.

Phone still in hand, Dad slowly took a seat in the chair behind him, seemingly unsettled by what he had just heard.

"Her uncle too?" he asked. After a minute of listening, he continued. "This all sounds very similar to how Janet has been acting."

Dad paused again before speaking.

"Okay, I think it's time we see a psychiatrist," Dad concluded.

I thought the conversation was over, but Dad remained on the line as my grandmother continued.

"Yes, what is it?" Dad asked. My grandmother must have said something shocking on the other end, because after a moment, he gasped as if he was in a state of disbelief.

"And?" he asked.

Dad went quiet. I saw the blood drain from his face as he was listening to whatever story Nanny was telling him.

"I can't believe she's never told me this." Dad paused again to compose himself and ended their conversation.

"Thank you, Marie," my father said, hanging up the phone. He looked over at me, shook his head a bit, and asked, "What are you watching, sweetie?"

"Care Bears," I said.

~

I was eight years old the first time I accompanied Mom to one of her therapy appointments. It was the spring of 1991, and Dad had taken the day off work to join us. Sam was at Aunt Francine's house being cared for since my parents felt she was too young to take part.

To me, as a young girl, the office seemed extremely large, much bigger than any other doctor's office I had been to. I sat in an oversized dark brown leather chair and the mahogany desk in front of me made me feel small, like an ant or a bug of some sort. The walls were lined with degrees from several institutions and tall plants were placed around the room to, from what I could guess, create a soothing atmosphere. Mom sat straight up in the matching chair next to mine, almost as if she were posing like a schoolgirl for the teacher, and Dad stood next to her, his arms crossed. Across from us sat Doctor Lantire in an even bigger chair, wearing large glasses and drinking something that smelled of lemon and herbs.

"Please take a seat, Greg," Doctor Lantire gestured toward the bench along the wall. "Would any of you like some tea?"

"No, thank you," my father said as my mother shook her head in unison.

"Very well," the doctor said. "I see you've asked Michelle to come along today."

I did not want to be there and was secretly hoping that the session would be quick. As I sat there quietly, I skeptically looked at him.

"Michelle, honey, we brought you along so Doctor Lantire can explain my disease to you," Mom said.

"Okay," I said cautiously.

"Michelle, your mom has what we call manic depression. She is sick. It is just as when you get a cold or the chicken pox, except this disease affects her mind," Doctor Lantire said, trying to explain Mom's disease to me using simple terms. Over the past two years, I had been reading articles about bipolar disorder, and though they were less medical, more eight-year-old-friendly, he was only reiterating what I already knew. He continued. "Everyone has what we call neurotransmitters in their brain and when they aren't working correctly, someone can show signs of mental illness, just like your mom."

"Okay," I said again, plainly and disinterested.

"Michelle, tell me. Do you ever notice that your mom is sad?" the doctor asked. "And I don't mean that she hurt her finger or stubbed her toe. I mean that she seems very sad."

"Um, I guess," I said, though I was well aware of what he was suggesting.

"That is what we call a depressive episode."

"Okay."

"And do you remember the time your mom covered the kitchen in bubbles and dish soap?" the doctor asked.

"Yes," I said, remembering back to that day. That was such a fun day for me and Sam.

"That is what we call a manic episode," Doctor Lantire explained.

"Okay."

"Do you want to share with me what happened that day?" Doctor Lantire asked.

I hesitated. I didn't expect that I would have to speak much during this session, nor did I want to. "I don't know. Mom let us play in the kitchen with bubbles," I said. "Sam and I had fun."

"I understand you had fun. But you also need to understand that this is not normal," he said. "It is fine to have a good time with Mom, but if something extreme like this happens again, you need to speak with an adult right away."

"Okay."

"This disease does run in families," Doctor Lantire said. "Your great uncle had it and so did your grandfather."

"Do you remember when I told you about Uncle Ned?" Mom asked.

"Yes," I said. I remember she told me never to go near him, especially if I was alone. I would come to find out years later when I was an adult that Uncle Ned undressed himself and crept into my mother's room in the middle of the night. Luckily, she woke from her sleep and screamed loud enough for the rest of the house to hear, and her older brother took care of the situation.

"I would like to add that the majority of mentally ill patients are not inherently dangerous," the doctor said.

"I know," I said, knowing my mother was definitely not dangerous.

"What your mom has can be controlled with medication and therapy," the doctor said. "So, if there's anything you feel like you need to talk about, we are all here for you."

Mom stepped in. "Do you want to talk about your feelings?" she asked.

Absolutely not! I thought. But I kept that to myself because I didn't want to trigger anyone. All I wanted was for this conversation to be over, so I responded with a simple, "I'm okay."

"Are you sure?" Dad asked.

"Yeah."

"Okay, thank you for coming here today, Michelle. I really appreciate you showing up," Doctor Lantire said.

"Michelle, please take a seat in the waiting room," Dad said. "We need to speak with the doctor for a bit longer."

I walked out of the room and sat down in a small chair next to the receptionist. She smiled at me with wide eyes, knowing I would be able to hear whatever was being said in the next room.

"We can't force her to talk," the doctor said. "You will just have to be open and ready when she wants to."

"I understand," Mom said.

"I think she gets it. She's a smart girl," Dad added.

"Is there anything else you would like to discuss with me today?"

"Not with Michelle here," Mom said. "Thank you."

My parents met me in the waiting room. They grabbed my hand and led me to the car. That was the first and last time I ever saw Doctor Lantire's office.

Two weeks later, Mom experienced a significant psychotic episode. It was unclear to me what exactly tipped her off, but after dinner, as Dad was cleaning the dishes, Mom started to wail. We all rushed to the living room to see her on her back sprawled across the floor reading the Serenity Prayer aloud while sobbing to herself. "God grant me the serenity to accept the things I cannot change," she cried, flailing about as Dad tried to calm her down. I stood next to Sam as we watched the event unfold, both of us speechless.

~

I had never seen a straitjacket before. As I peered through the large window, I remember it wasn't perfectly white, but tanned and wrapped around my mother, who was unconscious lying on a table. There we were, back in the hospital like we had been a few years ago, except this time, in a very different wing.

"Why is Mommy like that?" I asked, startling Dad from behind. I was mostly confused as opposed to worried or scared.

"Oh, sweetie, come with me. You aren't supposed to see that," Dad said. "Where is Aunt Francine?" Dad led me back to the waiting area. On the way, we saw Aunt Francine and Sam searching the hallways.

"Oh Michelle, there you are!" Aunt Francine called out.

"What happened?" Dad asked.

"I'm so sorry. I was coloring with Sam and when I looked up Michelle was gone," Aunt Francine explained. "How is Janet?"

"She's going in for shock therapy."

I took my sister's hand and walked with her back to the coloring books. I did not want her to see what was on the other side of the large window.

Chapter 6

The Beginning of the After

March 1992

When I was growing up in the 1980s and 90s, the stigma surrounding mental illness was especially strong. I never spoke about Mom's illness to my friends, or anyone for that matter. From what I gathered, my friends' parents were perfectly healthy and I didn't need to tell them my mother had been in and out of psychiatric hospitals most of my life.

For the past year, Mom remained on the medication prescribed by Doctor Lantire, but there were times when she would stop without notice. It was not like my father would, nor could, watch her take her medication throughout the day, and we always relied on Mom to make the decision. When she did stop, it would only take a few days until she started to show signs of irrationality or mania or deep depression, making it generally unsafe for me and Sam to be around her, especially when we were alone. In those instances, Dad would take us to Aunt Francine's or Aunt Gail's while Mom rested at home or, worst case, in the hospital where it could take weeks for her to recover. Sam and I would quickly adjust to our new schedule only for it to return to whatever normality we had weeks later.

Sam, who was now six years old, was at the tail end of her treatment and she had been slowly weaning off the medication. In about a year, she would stop chemotherapy altogether. Although this sounded promising, it also meant her body would have to fend for itself. I could tell Mom and Dad were anxious, growing outwardly tense as the days got closer. I would look at Sam though and didn't feel nervous—I knew she was a fighter.

Over the past four years, Mom poured most of her energy into Sam's health, rushing her to see the doctor if she was exposed to any sort of illness, while Dad focused on work, ensuring we would not lose the medical insurance that paid for the cancer treatments. It had been a harrowing few years of chemotherapy medication, spinal taps, and bi-weekly blood draws, but Sam's energy had improved dramatically. We were finally able to play together again like we did when we were much younger.

With Sam progressing positively, much of the family's focus shifted to my mother's illness, which took quite a toll on her and my father's relationship. The fighting between them started infrequently at first but then progressed to several times a week. I never understood exactly what they were arguing about, but it always seemed heated.

I was sitting on the couch doing homework one evening when the yelling started a few feet away from me in the hallway by the front door.

"You can't keep doing this! You can't keep spending money we don't have," my father said, his voice raised.

"Oh, come on, I saw this beautiful Chanel. Don't you love it on me?" Mom asked, showing off the new handbag around her arm.

Dad wouldn't let up. "We've been struggling with finances as is. Where do you think I'm getting the money to support your ridiculous shopping sprees?"

"Oh, it's just a bag, Greg," Mom said sarcastically, prancing away from him with her new possession as Dad reeled in disgust.

"Don't you dare walk away from me!" My father shouted in a way that made my mother stop in her tracks. He walked up to her and grabbed the bag from her arm. "I'm returning this."

"Oh, no you're not!" Mom hissed.

But Dad took the bag and stomped straight to the car. I ran to the window and watched him speed down the driveway, blasting rocks and dirt in his wake.

Mom stood there, stunned. "I can't believe he did that," she said to herself. Then, she noticed me by the window in the living room.

"I'm sorry you had to hear that," Mom said. She then changed the subject "How was school?"

I was relieved she didn't want to talk about the incident with my father. "Ms. Donatello gave us so much homework," I told her.

"Again? I don't understand these crazy teachers," Mom said humorously as though she and Dad didn't just have a fierce fight.

"Yeah." I forced a laugh.

It was clear that Mom's emotional instability and anger, combined with Dad's absence at home, his own temper, and his inability to address her bipolar illness were enough to tear their once-happy marriage apart. As the months went on, the fighting between my parents grew even more intense, and more frequent. If one got angry, the other leveled up their own anger and it continued until a giant, uncontrollable whirlwind of conflict ensued. Even a conversation in the kitchen could be heard clearly from my bedroom, so when they fought, it was loud enough to wake me from a dream. For weeks, I had been woken up almost every night.

"You're never home!" Mom wailed in anger. "It's impossible to live like this!"

"Janet, I have no idea what you're talking about!" Dad was defensive, but also angry.

I was nine years old, yelling fruitlessly over the side of the dark wooden railing on the second floor. "Mom, Dad, please stop! Please stop." But neither my mother nor my father heard my cries over their fury. As a younger child, I would have kept my mouth shut, but over the years, I learned from my parents that I should start screaming back.

I had been yelling down the stairs for a full five minutes with no response. At that point, I was fed up and took it upon myself to stop them by intervening. I stomped down the stairs, the carpet silencing my footsteps.

"Greg, you are losing it," Mom screamed. "You wish I would keep my mouth shut. I won't stay silent. Just get out!"

"You are delusional! I don't even know what you're saying anymore," Dad hissed. "I'm not leaving my own house. MY house." With that response, I heard a loud thump, and the shouting suddenly stopped.

"I'm trying to sleep. Are you done yelling at each other?" I asked with a sharp tone in my voice. My mother gasped when she saw me appear in the doorway. I walked into the kitchen and saw Dad lay there moaning with his hand on his head. I wasn't sure what happened, but it looked like he got hit with some sort of object that wasn't in plain sight. "Dad, why are you on the floor?"

"I'm okay, sweetie, but I think I need to leave the house for a while. I'll be back," he said, slowly rising and walking out the door.

I stormed into the kitchen. "What happened?" I demanded from my mother after my father left.

"Your father is a good man. We got into a fight. Everything will be okay." Mom paused. "How about we get you back to bed?" Mom followed me up the stairs, tucked me in, and walked out of my room.

I couldn't sleep though. I thought of the rainbow drawing I had given to Sam when we were younger; the precious, beautiful rainbow I would think of whenever my heart would start beating wildly. Down the mist of colors, Sam and I both slid holding hands, happy as can be with the sun shining over us. But this time, it didn't work. I stared at the white popcorn ceiling in my bedroom, my mind racing in despair.

The next afternoon, Dad returned.

"Michelle, can we talk for a minute?" he asked, standing in my bedroom doorway. I had just returned home from school and was about to start my schoolwork.

"Dad, I have to do homework."

He ignored my suggestion and walked into my room closing the door behind him. "The fighting between your mother and I has gotten out of hand and you should not have witnessed any of it," he said. "It won't happen again."

"Okay, I just hate hearing you both fight," I said.

"I know. I do too."

"It's okay. Can I do my homework now?" I tried to end the conversation, though the incident still left a bitter taste in my mouth.

"I'll see you later." Dad walked out of my room. I saw him hesitate on the top step before heading down to where Mom was sitting on the couch. I could hear their conversation from my room.

"Janet," Dad said.

"Greg, what happened to us?" Mom asked defeated.

"We can't keep doing this in front of the kids. We fight every night." Dad paused and then spoke again, uttering the words that would forever alter our lives. "I've made the decision to get a divorce."

I gasped in shock but remained quiet.

"What do you mean? Oh Greg, we can work through this, can't we?" Mom sounded desperate.

"It's been years of this. We have no chance of working through it anymore," Dad said more callously.

"Oh, you think I don't know you've been seeing someone else?" Mom said coldly.

"I'm not getting into this. Michelle is upstairs," Dad said. "You can stay in the house but I'm moving out tomorrow. This is over." He stood up and walked outside to work on his antique car, his way of disassociating from the chaos in his life.

I knew my parents had their issues as evidenced by the constant fighting, but I didn't truly understand the full significance of their struggles. The next morning, I was called downstairs and asked to take a seat on the couch next to Sam.

Sam and I sat close to Mom and listened to Dad speak. "Girls, I won't be around the house much anymore. This isn't your fault," Dad said with a gentle tone. "I am still here for you, and your mother will be as well. We love you both so much."

Mom didn't speak much, but when she did, all she mustered was, "We love you girls very much."

As we sat silently, Dad kept talking, but as he spoke, I noticed something—he never used the word "divorce". Strangely, I was not sad, not because I was happy my dad was leaving, but because I didn't quite understand the repercussions of divorce nor the financial and emotional hardships that would ensue. But I cried. I cried because I felt like I had to. I cried because I felt that's what children do when their parents divorce. Mom also cried, but for very different reasons.

When Dad finished his speech, he gave Sam and me each a kiss on the forehead and stood up slowly from the couch. He reached the door and picked up his suitcase.

Then, Sam screamed, her little voice quivering as she started to run toward the door. "Daddy, don't leave us!" Mom grabbed her and held her tight as my sister tried to break free.

"Come here, sweetie," Mom said, devastated.

Dad looked back at me and Sam for a quick moment with a pained but resolute expression on his face. Then he turned around and walked out the door.

~

For weeks following the separation, Mom was heartbroken and completely shut down. My mother fought hard for my father to stay, begging and pleading with him, and when he didn't respond to her, she turned to me for help.

"Michelle, can you call Dad again?" Mom asked, her voice tinged with longing.

"Mom, I don't know what else I can say to him." After weeks of this, I started to accept the fact that my father would not be coming home and there was nothing I could do to change it.

"Please? For me?" Mom begged.

"Okay, I'll try, Mom." I picked up the handset and placed it next to my ear, slowly spinning the numbers on the rotary phone one by one. As each number spun back to its original spot, I winced, not knowing what I was going to say to my father this time that would be any different from the last. I sat on the dining room carpet beside the credenza with my back leaning against the wallpaper. I had done this almost every night that month, begging my father to come home as Mom sat on the couch in the background crying. This time though, I realized I was no longer begging for myself, but only for my mother.

"Dad, Mommy is so upset. Can you please come home?" I pleaded.

"Sweetheart, we can't keep doing this. I love you girls so much, but I'm not coming home," he responded gently.

"Please, Daddy? Mommy misses you. I miss you."

"I know. I miss you too. I will see you on Tuesday for our visit though! We can go bowling." Dad was trying to re-direct my attention, which I easily picked up on, but I decided to use it as an out to get off the phone. I no longer wanted to beg—it was too emotionally draining.

"Okay, Daddy. I still miss you, but I'll see you Tuesday."

Just then, Mom unexpectedly approached me from behind and snatched the handset away from me. I looked up at her, almost scared at her hostility. "Greg, how can you keep living like this knowing what you're doing to this family?" Mom was desperate. "Please come home!"

I couldn't hear what my father said, but I immediately noticed how Mom's face changed. The pleading look faded, replaced by a sort of sad acceptance, as if Dad told her something she couldn't control. Mom had no choice but to allow the marriage to dissolve, and the phone calls stopped after that night.

~

Mom very clearly fell into an even deeper depression, experiencing waves of grief that caused her to either withdraw or lash out at us, and this time, Dad wasn't around to help. I took it upon myself to step in, handling it with the limited knowledge I had from previous bouts. Mom would start crying at arbitrary points during the day and night, with nothing in particular, at least outright, that would cause it.

A few nights went by. Mom, Sam, and I were having dinner, talking about our school day and Sam showed off a new book she checked out of the school library. Out of nowhere, Mom crouched over in her chair, her dinner spilling out of her mouth onto the floor as she cried. Sam placed her fork down and looked at me with a growing frown. I whispered to her, "It's okay" and grabbed Mom's hand to lead her upstairs to the bedroom. "Mom, let me get you to bed," I said gently.

"Oh, Michelle," Mom said as she walked up the stairs with tears down her cheeks. "I'm so sorry."

During her depressive episodes, the house duties and mental load now fell on me as Mom stayed in bed for days on end. Seemingly overnight, my childhood innocence hardened into a kind of pseudo-maturity. It was as if I had crossed an invisible threshold into a shattered new dimension at just ten years old. I was unexpectedly expected to take on a parental role even though I was still just a child desperately trying to navigate adolescence and develop my own identity. Yet as I was doing so, I was handed the impossible task of maintaining stability in a home with a mentally ill mother. Though I did not understand it at the time, my identity started to revolve around this new caregiver role as opposed to discovering what I liked or the type of person I wanted to become.

Not only was I forced to navigate Mom's illness, but I was now fully responsible for Sam's well-being. Although Mom was still physically able to care for us, she lacked the mental capacity to guide us into adulthood effectively; her moods shifted so easily that even the smallest bit of bad news could trigger an emotional breakdown or furious outburst. I had no choice but to accept my new role, and it left me, not only scared, but resentful.

"Sam! Did you do your homework?" I yelled from the kitchen one evening after school as I was washing the dishes that had been sitting in the sink all day. I turned the water off and drained the basin, using a towel to dry my hands. As I did, I noticed the leaves on the large oak tree in our backyard changing colors and the plants in the garden swaying in the crisp autumn breeze. It had been two months since Dad left, and I recently had my first birthday without him in the house.

"I'm working on it now," Sam shouted back from the dining room.

"Hey, listen, Mommy isn't doing too well," I said after joining her at the table. "I'll take Max for a walk. Can you feed him?"

"Yeah, sure."

"Thanks. Do you need help with that?" I asked, pointing to Sam's paper.

"Sure."

It was a simple first-grade exercise—Sam had to write the upper- and lower-case letter "G" a few times on lined paper.

Just then, Mom came down the stairs looking more refreshed than she had been in months. It looked like she had showered and put on a pair of jeans and a blouse, a nice change from her worn out pajamas.

"Hey, girls!" Mom sounded excited.

"Hi, Mom," I said. "You look nice."

"Thank you, my sweetheart," she said, coming over to give me a kiss on the forehead. "I think we should go for a walk!"

"Sorry, Mom, I have to finish my homework," Sam said.

"Yeah, I'm helping her through it," I added. "We should be done soon."

"Oh no you don't," Mom said playfully. "It's beautiful outside. Let's go sing with the birds." She started tweeting to herself, singing as though she knew the song, but I couldn't recognize the tune.

"Sorry, Mom, maybe another time," I said.

"Oh, to hell with you both," Mom said scornfully.

"What?" Sam said, confused, not fully understanding where her ill temper came from. I tried my best to shield Sam from Mom's angry outbursts, but it was only inevitable that she would witness them periodically.

"Nevermind," Mom said and walked off to the kitchen.

"Mommy seems angry," Sam said.

"It's okay, Sam," I said as I looked off, concerned. Mom experienced both highs and lows, though the medication prevented her lows from getting too depressive and her highs from turning manic. This time, though, it seemed as though Mom's slow-forming high was now coupled with irritability, a combination I was unfamiliar with. I had experienced Mom's anger before, but only during one of her lows. Now it surfaced when she was supposed to be happy—or at least appeared to be. Deep down though, I knew Mom wasn't happy at all, but deeply unsettled.

I entered the pantry after helping Sam write a few capital letters, hoping to get some sense of why Mom snapped at us. I stopped when I heard Mom on the phone with Aunt Francine. She was openly complaining.

"Fran, can you believe he walked out on us? His family, his girls," Mom wailed, but in a low enough voice hoping we could not hear from the dining room. She didn't notice I was standing at the doorway off the pantry.

"My life has completely flipped. How has this happened to me?" Mom continued venting.

This wasn't the first time I had overheard a conversation where Mom expressed her pain so openly. As a young girl, I could not yet understand why Mom was so broken and did not want to hear the blunt truth of what was happening in my own life, so I retreated. I went back to the dining room, sat next to my sister, and resumed helping with her homework. Rather than facing it head on, I was slowly distancing myself from any grief that crept into my life.

Chapter 7

Lost

After my father moved out, my relationship with him changed dramatically, and quickly. The two of us, who had been inseparable during my childhood years, had grown apart in the months after my parents' last fight. My resentment slowly grew when the consequences of the divorce became apparent. I blamed my father and felt bitter not only because he walked away from our family, at least according to my mother, but also because my mother was so irritable all the time. Confusion set in because even though Dad told me this was the right thing for me and Sam, everything felt wrong. Not only did I think my father was the cause of our family falling apart but I wanted the dad who had been with me every step of the way, as he had been when I was a little girl.

But that was never going to happen. I had witnessed him quickly moving on from the family we had previously formed, and in doing so, he unintentionally grew apart from me and Sam. It only took the night Dad left for me to realize he wasn't going to tuck me into bed and read me a story, suddenly a tradition of the past.

Dad was now living in a small town in Connecticut, though at the time, I wasn't sure why he moved so far away from Nutley. Even still, he visited me and Sam twice a week. Every Tuesday and Thursday after he got home from work, he would pick us up, always honking the car horn from the street and never coming to the door. He would then take us to my grandmother's house, the house he grew up in, on the other end of town. My grandmother was still teaching piano lessons at eighty years old but didn't mind the company as my grandfather passed away years prior. To get out of the house, Dad would usually plan an activity with us like bowling or mini golf to keep us entertained. I enjoyed the time I spent with my father, but it just wasn't the same as when he lived at home. Our relationship now felt forced.

It must have been at least four or five months of separation from Mom before Dad introduced me and Sam to his new girlfriend, but looking back, it felt like a week. Jillian was an intelligent woman in her early twenties, soft-spoken and the complete opposite of my mother. It seemed as though Dad was ready to start a new life with a young woman he met at work.

"Girls, I'd like you to meet my very good friend. Her name is Jillian," Dad said. "She will be coming around here more often."

"Nice to finally meet you, Michelle and Sam," Jillian said.

Sam and I were polite, the way we were taught to be. We didn't say much, but most likely because I don't think Sam understood what Dad meant by the word "friend". I knew, but detached myself from the situation, something that I trained myself to do. I smiled, walked to the couch and put in my headphones.

Jillian looked at my father and then continued with Sam. "Do you like to color? I have crayons."

"Sure," Sam said and the two of them walked over to the dining table. I turned the music up.

My father was not happy with my lack of engagement. "I'd like you to get to know Jillian," he said in a stern voice a few moments later.

"I'm listening to music," I replied flatly.

"Please, get up and talk to her," he said.

I was provoked. I looked him directly in his eyes and replied, "No."

And that's when the shouting started. My father wouldn't let up. He wanted me to talk to Jillian, even if it meant that I had to force a smile and pretend. I, on the other hand, refused to feign happiness just to appease my father who had upended my life in what felt like an instant. I didn't want to meet whoever this woman was. I wanted Dad back home.

This wasn't the first time my father yelled at me. He had raised his voice before, for example, when I didn't clean up after myself or get out of the house on time. But this argument was different— it was the first time I felt like I was fighting *for* my father rather than against him, and I didn't want to give in.

~

Back at home, Mom was not only depressed, but she also began acting erratically, often packing me and Sam up in our blue Oldsmobile without notice to go out for long drives to seemingly nowhere in particular. The car, though in need of repairs and some cleaning, generally fit its purpose and was overall reliable. On one such occasion, I had just returned from school and Mom was already leading Sam out to the car.

"Michelle, I'm glad you're finally back," Mom said. "Come on. We're going for a drive!" Mom seemed eager to leave the house, though I couldn't understand why.

"It's almost dinnertime. Where are we going?" Sam asked as she followed Mom down the stairs leading to the backyard, though she and I both knew the answer before the question was asked.

"I think we should just drive and take in the scenery around us," Mom responded.

"In New Jersey?" I quipped as I roughed up Max's head with my hands. He had been jumping up and down by my leg, excited to see me since I walked in the house.

"We'll take a drive west," she said. "I once drove out there long ago and the landscape by the Delaware Water Gap is beautiful, I promise."

"Okay," I said as I gave Max a kiss on his snout. My fifteen-pound white fluff-ball looked up at me with sad eyes, realizing I was leaving yet again. I then followed Mom and Sam out to the car knowing I had little choice.

Mom had driven for about two hours west past bare trees and rocky ridges that lined the cascading rivers below. Overhead, an ominous gray cloud cluster started rolling toward us, and the darkness of the sky made me feel apprehensive. It was a warm day for January, but still cold, and I knew the road could easily turn to ice if it rained.

"Mom, I think we should head back," I said nervously.

"Just a little further and then I'll turn around. There's a waterfall I want to show you," Mom said with a glaring expression, almost as if she could think of nothing else except this waterfall. "We can head back soon."

It wasn't long before the rain started beating against the car. The wipers weren't fast enough to see clearly out of the windshield, and Mom had to slow quite a bit due to the limited visibility. The two-lane road off the highway was wide enough to allow for a slow U-turn before we were able to reach our destination, and we were forced to head back home.

It wasn't another twenty minutes before the car started puttering, jerking back and forth before it made a complete stop on the side of the road. By this time, we had returned to the busier highway, but there were few cars on the road due to the storm and our location.

"Oh shoot!" Mom exclaimed, looking at the gas meter.

"Mom?" I asked.

"We just ran out of gas," Mom said. "I think there is a gas station a few miles that way." She said it matter-of-factly, neither appearing scared nor concerned, despite the fact we were stranded hours away from home on a road covered in darkness and rain. I couldn't determine whether she was masking her nerves or if she genuinely felt no worry at all.

I, on the other hand, felt the anxiety quickly overtake my body, and I turned suddenly quiet. I felt my heart race and stomach drop as I sat in the front seat facing the road. Sitting very still, I was almost scared to move because I felt that if I did, something very terrible would happen.

"We're going to have to hitchhike back to the station," Mom said. "Girls, come with me. I think I have an umbrella in the trunk." She opened the door to the rain pouring down.

The small umbrella barely covered the three of us as we huddled in the cold behind the back of the car, the red glow from the taillights casting light over our little waiting spot. Mom, as if she had done this before, reached her arm toward the highway, her thumb raised.

An unkempt, bearded man in overalls was the first to pull up in a rusty blue pickup truck. He looked like he had come straight from tending livestock.

"Hi, are you stuck?"

I glanced in his direction and quickly looked over at my mother with wide eyes, indiscreetly shaking my head "no".

Mom picked up on my hesitation. "Oh, thank you but we have someone coming to pick us up in the next few minutes." Mom waved him off. "Drive carefully!"

"Are you sure?" he asked.

"Yes, I think that's him right there." Mom looked at another vehicle headed in our direction. Before this vehicle reached us, the man sped off.

"Mom, I don't like doing this," I said once he was gone.

One by one, cars raced by as the rain continued to fall. It took another fifteen minutes before a large semi-truck pulled up next to us. On the side of the trailer was a name that I couldn't quite make out, but I could tell it was one of a large well-known company. Though still uneasy, I felt this was probably the safest option.

The trucker was stocky and wore a baseball cap that covered the top half of his face, but his smile was friendly enough to where I felt a bit relieved. "So, what happened?" he asked.

"I was so distracted by the rain that I forgot to fill the tank. Would you mind driving us to the gas station?" Mom asked. "It should only take a few minutes."

"I think I can spare a few moments to help you and your daughters, ma'am," he said with a slight southern accent. "My name's Jim."

"Thank you so much, Jim. We really appreciate this."

Sam and I sat in the cab directly behind the driver and Mom sat next to him in the front seat. When we reached the gas station, Mom filled up a small gas can with fuel and Jim drove us back to our stranded car. He hung around until the gas tank was filled and drove off into the night.

~

I felt my life slowly unraveling. When I was with my mother, it was unpredictable, erratic, and when I was with my father and his girlfriend, it felt stressed, unfamiliar. My relationship with my father deteriorated even further as he continued to pressure me to welcome Jillian into my life when all I wanted was him. Then, the literal bomb went off.

It was the afternoon of February 26, 1993, and I was sitting at my desk listening to my teacher ramble on about plant ecosystems. It was two days before Sam's birthday, so my mind was more focused on the party my mother planned for the weekend than learning about life sciences. As I stared at the clock, my teacher was interrupted by the principal who walked into the room.

"Michelle Hanes, come with me," she said.

Principal Cartright was an older woman, stout and friendly, but would cast a stern shadow when she suspected trouble. She was frowning when she called for me. I was a good student, so hearing her say my name in a more serious tone felt peculiar to me and I questioned why I would have to go to her office.

"Your mom called and she will be picking you and Sam up shortly," she said.

"Oh, okay," I said breathing a sigh of relief. But then, as we were walking to the main office, I realized something must have happened. "What is this about?" I asked.

"I think it's best you speak with your parents."

Not long after, Mom came to get me and Sam from the main office. "I'm so sorry, Janet. Is Greg okay?" the receptionist asked. She must not have known of the separation.

"He is fine." Mom sounded stressed. I felt reassured knowing there was nothing wrong with my father but confused that my mother was picking us up for something related to him. "I wanted my girls home with me today though."

"Of course," she said. Sam and I looked at each other with puzzled eyes.

The three of us exited the building and entered the car. "What's going on?" I asked Mom as soon as I closed the door behind me.

"Nothing, sweetheart. It's Friday and I just wanted to pick you up early!" Mom said, trying her best to sound genuine, but I could tell something was up.

"Ooh! Can we make hot chocolate when we get home?" Sam asked, happy to be out of school.

"What do you mean? They mentioned something about Dad," I interrupted.

"Your father is fine," she said. "You'll see him Tuesday. I just wanted to see you both." Mom seemed sad, almost scared, but she didn't let on any more than that.

When we got home, we did nothing out of the ordinary. Mom, Sam, and I played a few board games and watched a movie cuddled up on the couch. It appeared she needed some sort of comfort, and though I didn't pry, I knew there was something she wasn't telling me.

I learned not long after that Dad, who was working on the eighty-seventh floor of the World Trade Center building in downtown Manhattan that year, lived through the 1993 terrorist attack of the North Tower. My father recalled the story, though he didn't go into the grim details until years later when I was much older.

Shortly before he left for lunch with a few coworkers, my father felt a short-lived yet distinct rumble beneath him. Then, the lights flickered. Knowing something was wrong, but not exactly sure what, he walked with swiftness in his step to the stairwell, knowing not to get into an elevator. He climbed down nine floors, at which point he noticed the gray smoke that started to billow up quickly, almost as if a thick rain cloud was rising beneath him. Moments later, the lights blew out, and it was so black that my father couldn't see his own hand that was spread only a few inches in front of his face.

Then, more hastily, he descended the next seventy-eight floors in complete darkness and made his way to safety on the outside. His face covered in soot, he walked as fast as he could to Penn Station, where he caught a train not to us, but to Jillian.

Chapter 8
The Walk I Took Alone

November 1994

It was now almost two years since Jillian and my father started dating and the relationship between me and my father remained fragile as we grew increasingly distant. Jillian seemed nice and she didn't fight with Dad like my mother did, but at twelve years old, I didn't want stability, I wanted my father home and the chaos back.

I didn't know who to turn to or who to confide in, so I focused on the only thing I could—my studies. Up until fourth grade, my marks were good, but by the end of fifth grade, they were perfect. I had just entered sixth grade and had already read through my entire science textbook. Literature, science, math—they all became an escape, a way to dissociate from the shattered world around me, and I spent most of my time alone in my bedroom after school.

I tried to make friends, but it was difficult for me. Sixth grade was the beginning of the final year of elementary school, a year where I was supposed to be the leader, the oldest class, someone the younger kids could look up to. But what it turned out to be was the beginning of a year of bullying. I didn't know how to stand up for myself and crouched away anytime someone made a snide remark or laughed at me on the playground. To me, defending myself meant losing friends, or whoever else was in my life.

It was a sunny autumn day in November. The leaves were turning orange and yellow and the ones that had fallen left a thin layer on the school grounds. My mother had just let Sam off at the front of school where she lined up for second grade, while I was being driven around the back near the older students. Outside the car door, I opened *The Road to Oz*, a book I had been waiting to read all morning.

Before I closed the door, I heard my mother speak. "You look like a nerd, Michelle. Keep your head up."

I put my book away. The last thing I wanted to do was look like a book nerd. Then, before I walked away, she shouted out the window. "Why don't you invite your friends over to play later?"

I did what she asked and after school, I found myself in my bedroom with two girls who I had known since kindergarten. I considered Priscilla and Kate to be good friends; they were the ones I would invite to birthday parties and have sleepovers with. Something about them changed though since I had seen them before the holiday break, and they seemed different, more intimidating. They were laughing at something in my room, but I couldn't quite see what it was until they moved. There, behind them were the stick figures Sam and I drew on the wall together. The laugh wasn't friendly though—they were mocking the drawing.

"What is this?" I heard Kate ask.

"Just a stupid drawing," Priscilla said.

"We should color over it," Kate suggested. "I'm sure there are crayons around here somewhere."

"No, please don't," I said timidly from across the room.

"Okay, fine," Priscilla said. "I have a better idea."

Then, without hesitation, Priscilla walked to my wooden dresser, opened the top drawer and started tossing my underwear all over the room before I could even begin to comprehend what was happening.

"What are you doing?" I asked, utterly embarrassed.

She looked down at the mess, laughing. Then in a sarcastic tone, she continued, "Oh no! We need to clean this up!" And the next thing I knew, she and Kate, who had also been laughing, picked up a pile from the floor, opened the window, and tossed them out. There my undergarments flew, into the trees and along the front lawn for all my neighbors to see.

Years of stories and sleepovers suddenly turned into ridicule and harassment. I thought back to the past few months but couldn't understand why they were taunting me so much. *Maybe my mother was right—maybe I was a nerd. Was I really that awkward? Or worse—maybe they found out about my mother, the mental patient?* I could never have asked that though and determined maybe I didn't deserve friends.

For the rest of that year, I barely spoke to Priscilla and Kate, and they formed their own clique, one that I was not included in. That night at bedtime, I turned off the lights, crawled under the covers, and cried.

~

About two weeks before Christmas that year, Dad and Jillian brought me and Sam out to their favorite restaurant. We sat in the booth that we always did, and the waiter came over to take our order. The lighting was dim, and I could barely see the menu. I didn't need to though because I would always order the same thing.

"The spareribs, please?" I said after everyone else ordered their food.

"Sure, is that it for you all?" the waiter asked.

"Yes, thank you," my father said.

"I'll be right back with your drinks," the waiter said and walked away.

"Well girls, we have some news!" Dad said. He was excited and I could see the gleam in Jillian's eyes as well.

I ignored him and instead thought about the game we always played at restaurants where someone would flick the quarter from their end of the table and try to land it on the opposite edge.

"Can we play the quarter game?" I asked. I had an inkling about what they were going to tell us.

"Sure, but after we tell you we are getting married!" Dad exclaimed, putting his arm around Jillian.

"Congratulations," I said flatly and grabbed a quarter from my pocket. Sam didn't speak.

"Thanks!" Jillian exclaimed. "And of course you will both be in the wedding."

"Sounds great," I said, and placed the quarter down on the table, preparing to flick it. I was slowly learning that I, in fact, could play pretend.

Over the next few days, I was tasked with breaking the news to Mom, yet another emotional pile of garbage thrown onto my plate. I didn't really know how to approach the conversation, so I just blurted it out one day after school.

"Mom, Dad's getting married," I said.

"What?"

"Dad proposed to Jillian."

"Are you serious? What am I? Just trash now, Michelle?" Mom said harshly.

"I don't know what to say, Mom." I tried to keep my emotions in check, afraid how she might react. But then she began to weep loudly, and I sat motionless, unsure of how to navigate her unresolved trauma. "Mom, stop," I begged.

"Oh, you are just like him," Mom snapped angrily.

With that, I huffed off to the living room. I could tell Mom was upset, but her anger toward me made me pull back, and at that moment, I felt no sympathy for her. I opened my science textbook and started my homework without a second thought.

Mom didn't have many others to confide in—her sisters were happily married and couldn't understand what she was going through. There was, however, her sister-in-law, my Aunt Bea, with whom Mom felt comfortable talking to. I'm not sure why, but I think it had to do with her pragmatic, straightforward attitude.

"He proposed," Mom said to Aunt Bea as soon as she picked up the phone. Mom was more angry than upset, at least that's what I gathered from my spot on the couch.

Mom paused as Aunt Bea responded. Then she continued. "I'm heartbroken. It's been two years, Bea, but I still can't help feeling resentful. Was our marriage perfect? No. But did he love me? I know he did," Mom said. "That's what makes this so much harder." She wasn't attempting in any way to speak quietly.

Mom paused again and then spoke. "Michelle told me…" Her voice drifted off. She abruptly continued. "Hey, listen, I'm sorry to cut you off. I need to talk to her."

I quickly picked up the remote and turned on the television because one, I didn't want Mom thinking I was listening in, and two, to avoid whatever conversation we were about to have.

"Hey," Mom said as she entered the room. "I'm sorry about before. I'm sure this is hard on you too."

"I'm fine, Mom," I responded curtly, my eyes never leaving the television screen. I'd rather feel angry than sad. "Jillian is fine."

"Okay. Do you want to talk about it?"

"No. I'm fine."

"Okay," Mom said and walked out.

But I wasn't fine. I was aching as deeply as my mother, yet had no way to express it, afraid that any hint of my own emotion would set her's off. Because of this, our relationship suffered. As hard as I tried to maintain some semblance of a family, even if it was just me, Sam, and Mom, I was too emotionally fragile to take on such responsibility. I tried as hard as I could though to keep the family unit together, and to me, that meant not speaking up.

Later that night, Sam, Mom, and I ate dinner peacefully and not a word was said about the upcoming wedding.

~

Dad's marriage was difficult for me. They wed the spring of the following year, and I had to accept a new extension of my life with a woman only eleven years older than me. Jillian felt more like a sister, or a friend, than my stepmom, and yet I was expected to obey her as I did my father, assuming the role of a child on one end, while taking the role of the parent on the other with my mother. It was confusing for me. I couldn't just switch one off and turn the other on, something I was constantly expected to do.

By this time, Mom and Dad only spoke when the topic was related to me or Sam, and even then, they battled, often in front of us. I knew my parents were never going to get back together, but to see that they couldn't even be in the same room together, tore me apart.

Unlike my relationship with Mom, where I stayed silent during emotional moments, I became increasingly outspoken with Dad. I longed for the life we used to have, and I hoped that, if I caused a bit of chaos, he might retreat from his relationship with Jillian and pay more attention to me and Sam.

The anxiety that had begun in childhood had intensified, and I now had significant trouble sleeping. Some nights, I managed only three or four hours of sleep as I was constantly worrying about losing friends or failing an exam. I continued to do well in school, however, but it was as if I needed to be perfect, to prove to myself that something, anything, was under my control.

It was the summer of 1996, and I was thirteen years old. By this time, my grandmother on my father's side passed away, so Dad and Jillian purchased her house in Nutley and settled in. Every other weekend, we'd either sleep there or, during the summers, we would head to our beach house out on Oak Beach, Long Island. This particular weekend was supposed to be perfect weather, so Dad, Jillian, Sam, and I piled into the car and made the three hour drive out to Oak Beach.

I knew we were close to the house when we exited off the high-traffic Meadowbrook Parkway and hit the more vacant Ocean Parkway which extended about fifteen miles east across the southern peninsula of Long Island. At the far end of Ocean Parkway, there was a roundabout which would either lead travelers to Robert Moses State Park to the south or back to the main island in the north. The bustling town of Babylon on the main island is where we would do most of the food shopping for the weekend.

About two thousand feet before reaching the roundabout at the far east end, we would make a right turn off Ocean Parkway. We'd then head back west onto a much narrower, more deserted road leading to the house. The first one hundred feet were paved, but the rest was rocky and had not been maintained in probably more than fifty years.

The house had been in our family for three generations before Dad inherited it from his mother. It was painted a deep red and situated directly on the beach overlooking the inlet that connected the Great South Bay with the Atlantic Ocean. As a child, I never understood why they called the side that faced the bay the "front" of the house, but looking back, I now see why. The view of the water was by far the most prominent feature.

The inside was filled from floor to ceiling with antiques and old furniture, and the main source of light was from the sun that shone through the six large windows in the dining room at the front of the house. Walled off from the living and dining rooms was the white-tiled kitchen where, if I looked closely in the tiny corner crevices, I could find a small bit of rust peeking through the linoleum. The sunroom filled with dusty record players and old books was off to the side of the dining room, and upstairs, there were four moderately sized bedrooms which smelled ever so potent of the mothballs that occupied the dresser drawers. Heat lingered in the house, cooled only by the bay breeze drifting through the windows, and a single window-unit air conditioner in the living room.

The beach, covered in small broken seashells, led up to the bulkhead separating the water from the property. On the other side, a set of stairs dropped about eight feet down to the water where Sam and I would swim and hunt for clam shells. Off to the right was a strip of land that continued out about a quarter of a mile. Lined with sand dunes, it was where the few annual visitors to Oak Beach set up blankets and umbrellas to bask in the sun. At the far end of the strip was a sort of cul de sac where the south side—the part hidden from view of the house—opened up to the ocean. I was told never to swim there due to the rough currents that often formed dangerous whirlpools. The beach was generally quiet as most visitors to the area traveled to the more popular Jones Beach to the west or Robert Moses to the east.

Because we arrived late at night, I was exhausted. Sam and I dropped our suitcases in the bedroom we shared and changed into pajamas. I then grabbed the woven blanket off the bed and walked down to the living room where the four of us would be watching a movie, as we did every night at Oak Beach.

"What are we watching?" I asked.

"Since we didn't get a chance to go to Blockbuster, we'll have to choose from the movies we have here," Dad said. "I see *Lion King* or *Arthur*."

"*Lion King*!" Sam and I shouted in unison. We were still young, and Grandma's favorite movie was not our first choice.

Dad put the tape into the VCR and left for the kitchen to make popcorn. Sam and I settled in at one end of the couch, while Jillian made herself comfortable at the other. Dad returned with two bowls of popcorn, handing one bowl to me and Sam, and taking the other for himself and Jillian. It wasn't a surprise Dad chose to sit next to Jillian, but for some reason, I was hoping it would be different this time, that he would want to sit next to me and Sam instead.

I felt an immediate rush of sadness wash over me. The pull Jillian had on my father had been tearing me apart for years. I tried my best to adjust to their relationship, to pretend in whatever way I could, but it was difficult. I didn't know how to effectively handle my emotions, nor did I have anyone I felt comfortable confiding in. I didn't speak up that night and tried my best to keep up the facade that we were a happy family even though all I wanted to do was scream.

The next morning, after another sleepless night filled with anxious thoughts, I decided I would say something.

"Hey, Dad," I said as I walked downstairs into the kitchen. Jillian was in the shower while Sam was playing solitaire at the dining room table.

"Hey, kiddo, what's up?"

"I was thinking we could go to town and get ice cream tonight," I suggested.

"Ooh yes!" Sam said, overhearing our conversation.

Dad responded, "That's a great idea! Jillian was saying how much she wanted to try 'The Scoop'."

"Oh. I was hoping *we* could go…just you, me, and Sam?" I asked, my heart dropping.

"No, Michelle. We've talked about this. That's not how we are going to do things. Jillian is part of our life now and she's going to join us."

"I really want it to be just us tonight. Please?" I begged.

"No. Jillian will be coming along," Dad reiterated, more strongly this time.

"Okay, fine, nevermind then! I'm not going!"

"You are not allowed to talk to me like that," Dad said, raising his voice.

With that, I stomped off to my bedroom and slammed the door. Then, I let it out.

The emotions—anger, fear, panic—building up inside of me since Jillian came into the picture washed over me and I cried silently on my bed so as not to draw any attention to myself. Dad had fallen in love again and he protected Jillian the way he used to protect me. I felt powerless, useless. I felt abandoned.

Sam entered my room soon after. "Hey, want to go out to the water and search for some clams with me?"

"I'm not really in the mood. Can you get out please?" I said, brushing her off as I wiped a tear away angrily.

Sam didn't leave though. "I'm not going back out there without you."

"I can't stand it. Why does she always have to be around?"

"I know," Sam said. "But we can't do anything about it, and I hate when you and Daddy fight."

"I don't know, Sam." I stood up. "I think I need some air."

"You know Daddy's going to talk to you right?" Sam knew how our fights would always pan out. Dad would sit me down and apologize for yelling but would never get to the root of the problem. That was up to me to figure out.

"I know." I paused. "Before he does though, I'm going to go for a walk. Do you know where my CD player is?"

"I think I saw it in the sunroom. Do you want me to come with you?" Even at ten years old, she tried.

"No, but I'll come clamming with you when I get back?" I suggested.

"Definitely!"

I grabbed my CD player, threw in a Nirvana album and headed for the front door, brushing past my father. "I'll be back," I said to him as I let the screen door slam shut behind me.

I had to cross the neighbor's front yard to reach the beach strip, but they never seemed to care. They've been neighbors for as long as I could remember, and we all got along well. I waded down by the water, letting my feet get wet to cool me from the harsh summer heat.

It took me about ten minutes to get to the end of the strip, and on the way, I passed two women basking in the sun, a man walking his dog, and a mother and father flying kites with their children. Then I turned the corner into the more secluded area that faced the harsher ocean. I was alone in my spot—it was close enough to the house yet far enough to escape everything going on in my life.

I sat down on a dune between two patches of tall grass, headphones still in my ears. The clouds drifted above, perfectly puffy in the blue sky as a swift breeze blew my hair off to the side. I threw it up into a ponytail, and leaned against the hill of sand, closing my eyes for a moment, trying to calm my body from the anger and anxiety I felt.

Just then, two young men approached and leaned over me. I only opened my eyes because the dark shadow they cast over me had shielded me from the sun. They weren't old enough to have graduated high school, but it looked as though they were at least upperclassmen in one of the nearby schools. One was tan, his light brown hair sweeping across his pronounced forehead, the other light-skinned with curly dark hair and deep brown eyes. Both, attractive.

"Hi, I'm David and this is Ian. What are you listening to?" the tan one asked as he moved the hair out of his eyes.

"Nirvana." I removed the headphones from my ears. I was slow to speak because I was shy, but I felt mildly curious. I didn't normally talk to other boys, but these two intrigued me.

The other boy spoke. "Interesting. So, what are you doing out here all by yourself?" Ian asked, his curls flowing in the wind.

"I'm just hanging out, getting away for a few minutes," I responded, blushing.

"Do you live on this beach?" David asked.

"My dad has a house down that way." I pointed toward the house. "We visit a lot during the summer."

"We live close by too. Do you want to come for a walk with us?" David asked. "We're headed toward Gilgo Beach." He pointed in the opposite direction from the house. I was interested, but nervous about straying too far away.

"Oh, I don't think my dad…" I started, using my father as an excuse.

"It's not that far, I promise. A few of us are just hanging out on the beach. You don't have to come if you don't want to," Ian said. Then he smiled. "But I think I'd like to have you there."

With that, I became even more attracted to him. *He wanted me there?* This was something I hadn't felt in a long time—a sense of belonging.

"Okay, maybe I can come for a little," I said. "But I have to be back in an hour. I promised my sister I'd go clamming with her."

"Sure, no problem. I'll walk you back," Ian said. And with that, I was excited for a new adventure.

The three of us started down the beach and it soon grew eerily quiet as the noise and laughter from the beachgoers at Oak Beach faded away. There was no one else in sight and an uneasiness settled over me.

"You know what? I think I need to go back to my dad's," I said, changing my mind.

"No, no. Don't worry," Ian said. He stopped, grabbed my hand, and leaned in to kiss me. As he did, he pulled my head toward his so I had no choice but to reciprocate. As we kissed, he pulled me over to the nearby dune off to the side of the shoreline.

I had never kissed a boy before, so the feeling of another boy's lips brushing up against mine was new to me. I once received a peck on the cheek from my sixth-grade boyfriend, Danny, on the playground, but that was the extent of my experience.

I always imagined my first real kiss to be magical, something out of a Disney movie I had watched many times. But this, this was anything but magical. I felt uncomfortable and tried to pull away, but Ian kept pulling me back while David sat close to the water, scanning the area, almost as if he was keeping a lookout for witnesses.

A surge of panic overtook me. I considered fighting, but Ian and David were much bigger, stronger, and faster than I was. So, instead, I tensed up to the point where I couldn't move willingly and just did what was told. Ian, continuing to kiss me, took my hand as if he wanted to hold it, but then, before I realized what was happening, he forced it down into his pants. As he did, he untied the string of his sweatpants and I felt his hand on mine, guiding the repetitive movements. I didn't stop for fear of what they would do to me, so I kept going until it was over and I was finally able to pull away.

"You're really pretty," Ian said. "Do you still want to come with us?"

The strange thing is, and what made me feel a great sense of shame in the moment, was that I *did* want to go with them. I didn't even know their last names, but I was a thirteen-year-old girl just trying to fit in. I didn't have many friends at home and the ones I did seemed fleeting. To me, whatever Ian did was normal—I didn't know anything different.

I made my decision though. "I think I'm going to head back now."

"Okay, maybe we'll see you around," Ian said as he and David walked off. I could hear them laughing with each other in the distance.

After taking a few minutes to stare off into the vast ocean, I turned away from the direction they were headed. I began the walk back with my head down.

I didn't quite understand what had just happened. I wasn't angry, I wasn't scared, I was just confused. So many questions raced through my mind, it was hard for me to keep track of any of them. *I didn't have sex, so was I raped?* I learned that rape was sex without consent, but this wasn't sex. *Or was it?* And Ian was a nice guy. He made me smile and feel giddy inside. *Anyone who could do that couldn't be a bad person, right?* Maybe I was making too big a deal of it. It's not like I was hurt in any way—I felt fine physically. And after thinking about it, I never said "yes", but I never said "no" either. *Should I have spoken up?* In the moment, it felt impossible though. *Maybe I should stop thinking about it altogether?*

Maybe this was all my fault.

The jumbled thoughts overwhelmed me, leaving no clear sense of anything. But one thought stood out, and it was a big piece of the puzzle that I couldn't quite fit into place—I knew I didn't want to do what I had done.

At thirteen years old, still just a child, I was sexually assaulted by a stranger.

~

In the end, I knew I wouldn't dare tell a soul. This was something I would bury deep inside, something I would try hard to forget. I had already spent years of my life figuring things out on my own, and I could add this to the list.

I walked along the dunes back around the cul de sac to the old red house. I pushed the front door open, put my CD player on the table, and didn't say a word as I hugged my father tightly. That is, until I apologized.

Chapter 9
The Shape of Quiet

June 1997

As I reflect on that day, I think about why I stayed silent, why I didn't tell anyone about the assault at Oak Beach. I suspect it was due to a few factors, though I can't pinpoint one in particular. For one, the deep embarrassment, the shame for what I had done, devoured me. I was totally disgusted with myself. Plus, what would I have said anyway? I didn't even have a name for what happened, and there was no way I was going to describe it to anyone else.

Second, I didn't know *who* to tell. I had one of three options at the time: Dad, Mom, or Sam. Though I don't know how anyone would have truly responded, I can only imagine the reaction from each. I assumed my father would have gotten angry at me for leaving the house, saying something along the lines of, "Well, you brought this upon yourself." Plus, he didn't keep anything from Jillian, and I didn't want to have to confide in her with any of this. My mother, on the other hand, would not have gotten angry, at least at me, but rather, I pictured her weeping and then cursing off my father. To me, this was the last thing I needed. The only person I would have felt comfortable disclosing this information to was Sam, but at ten years old, I felt she was too young to understand or offer any sort of comforting reflection. I resolved to tell no one.

~

It was one year after the incident at Oak Beach, and I had just graduated eighth grade. During middle school, I made friends and started dating, mostly boys from nearby towns. Both my friendships and relationships were short-lived though, and it seemed the assault created a distorted sense of what was normal in a relationship for me. I didn't feel valued and anytime I felt unsafe, I pulled away as a form of survival. I refused to acknowledge any shame, though I felt it deeply, and had concluded that this is who I was now.

Sam, it seemed, was my only constant.

It was summer, and Sam and I were home from school for the next three months. Mom was downstairs cooking dinner, and I had just opened the door to the bathroom.

"This is great news! I'm so excited!"

I jumped back a bit when I saw Sam, standing alone with a piece of notebook paper in hand. She looked as if she was rehearsing lines in front of the mirror.

"What in the world are you doing?" I asked confused, but also slightly entertained.

"I'm practicing what I'm going to say to Daddy and Jillian when we see them next," Sam explained.

"What do you mean?" I asked, taking a moment to think. Then Sam looked at me with a knowing look. I quickly caught on, and my tone suddenly changed. "Wait, does this have to do with the baby?"

"Yeah, I mean, can you believe Jillian's pregnant?"

"I know, but why are you practicing what you're going to say to them?"

"Because Mom still misses Dad and it's so hard to be happy, Michelle. If I slip and tell them how I really feel, then I'll get in trouble," Sam explained. "You know, like you do all the time!"

"Yeah, well, I have no problem telling them how you really feel if you want me to. But I get it," I said. "Let's keep this between us though. I don't think Mommy can handle this right now."

"I agree." Sam put the piece of paper into her backpack.

Later that night, as Mom was tidying Sam's room and packing her bag for the next day, the piece of notebook paper fell out onto the floor. Mom picked it up, read the first few lines, and dropped to the floor.

~

Jillian gave birth three days after my birthday in November of that year when I turned fifteen and entered my first year of high school. I recall being excited about my new sibling, to have a baby in the house, but that excitement was strongly curtailed by my mother's depression caused by it. And though I was anticipating the new arrival, I witnessed how my father had grown even further apart from the family we used to have, pouring most of his energy into Jillian and newborn preparations.

During that time, as I yearned for the relationship I'd once had with my father, I found solace in a budding connection with Mom who seemed to feel a similar type of longing. I was there to comfort her, offering a sort of silent empathy, and in doing so, our bond deepened. Neither of us ever spoke up about how we were feeling, but I stayed close by her side, taking time with her to enjoy hobbies, or watch movies together. She even taught me how to sew with her Singer.

It was October of that year, one month before Jillian gave birth. "Mom, they scored!" I shouted from her bedroom under the brown floral comforter of the king-size bed.

"Oh, of course I missed it! Who scored the run?" Mom asked, running back from the bathroom. She and I had been spending almost every night lying in bed watching the Yankees after Sam went to sleep. It was an easy way to connect without talking about anything other than baseball.

"Chili Davis," I answered. "Is that really his name?"

Mom chuckled. "I can't believe they pulled through after being down by five runs. But it's time for bed."

"Can I sleep in here again? Please?"

"Of course," Mom responded, even though I was a grown teenager and fully expected to sleep in my own room, at least by typical standards.

I smiled, pulled the covers over my head and drifted off to sleep. I felt safe sleeping next to my mother, but it was not enough to keep me from my nightmares. They were always the same—terrifying. In this one, I struggled to escape something, though I couldn't tell exactly what—I just knew I needed to run. But I couldn't. I was stuck. Stuck in the thick, consuming mud that pulled me back from whatever freedom I craved.

I jolted awake, my heart racing, my back wet from sweat. I turned to my side and found my mother sobbing quietly to herself. I didn't move, not because I didn't want Mom's pain to fade away but because I wanted to protect myself from feeling whatever pain she felt too.

The next morning, I quietly slipped out of bed so as not to stir Mom awake. I glanced over, noticing Mom's closed, but puffy eyes, and my stomach started to sink with a feeling of sadness. Before the feeling completely took over, I refocused my thoughts on my geometry exam later that day.

I was prepared for the test, but what I thought about most was Matt, the boy who sat next to me in class freshman year. He had scruffy blond hair, blue almond-shaped eyes, and a toothy grin, one that was warm and genuine. When Matt smiled at me the first day of class, my heart took off in a flutter. I was still shy though, and anytime I glanced in his direction, I would feel my face turn bright red. Speaking to him would have exposed my feelings, and I knew I could never let that happen.

Not only was I shaped by what had happened at Oak Beach, I also lacked my mother's guidance when it came to relationships. I had to figure it all out on my own, as I had to in most other areas of my life. I had grown cautious around other boys, yet something about Matt made me feel safe. He seemed shy too—nothing like Ian or David—and although I found trusting other people difficult, I continued to long for closeness with someone else.

I opened my closet, stared at the few clothes I owned, and wondered what to wear. I recalled one of the cheerleaders wearing a denim skirt the day before, strolling the halls confidently, smiling at everyone who passed. I wished I could have had that same level of self-assurance. I chose blue shorts with a light-yellow T-shirt—not a perfect match, but close enough.

Nutley High School was a short walk from our home, as long as I cut through the park down the street from where I lived. Today, I was early, and the sun was shining, so I didn't rush as I strolled down the path that led from the east end of Nutley to the west. I was five minutes from school when Matt startled me.

"Hey, Michelle!" Matt looked like he had been running to catch up with me, his face red from the sprint, his hair perfect.

I tried to remain cool, but my beating heart quickly sent a warm flush to my cheeks. I managed to let out a smile, but the words were stuck in my throat.

"Are you ready for Mr. Flint's exam today?" Matt asked when I failed to respond. "I was studying all night."

"Um, yeah. I guess so." The more eloquent words forming in my mind did not translate to my lips.

"Yeah, I don't know what I'm saying. You're always ready and ace all your tests," Matt said. "I actually…I was thinking maybe you could help me for my biology exam next week?" He blurted the words out as if he were fully expecting a rejection.

My eyes lit up as I spoke. "Um, yeah…"

"If you're busy, don't worry about it…" Matt cut me off, turning the exchange into a sweetly awkward dance.

"No. I mean yes, yes, I can help you. I'm free Saturday," I said with a smile as we continued our walk toward school.

"Perfect! We can do it at the library. I'll bring snacks."

"Ooh, snacks!" I joked.

Matt laughed. "I make a mean Chex Mix."

We walked the rest of the way together and I felt a surge of euphoria that I had never felt before.

When I got home from school that day, my face was glowing and the smile from that morning never left my face. I walked through the front door and up the stairs to my bedroom. I dropped my backpack on the floor and sprawled out onto my bed, dreamy and light. I was about to open my diary, ready to spill my heart onto the page, when a faint knock rapped on the door.

Mom walked in looking sad, broken. It only took a quick second, but my smile melted away.

"Hi, Mom, I had a really good…" I was hopeful as I started speaking, but was quickly cut off by Mom's moan, a sign that I recognized right away. I changed subjects. "Have you been taking your medication?" I asked. I didn't notice any of her symptoms the night before but sometimes they came on suddenly.

There was only silence.

My heart sank as I hesitated, knowing what this meant. The few moments it took to process my thoughts passed quickly, and I made my decision. I picked up the phone and called Aunt Francine. Within the hour, Mom was on her way to Doctor Lantire's office, while Sam and I were taken to stay at Aunt Gail's for the weekend so that Mom could get the help she needed.

Before I left the house, I made another phone call, this time to Matt. My nerves were rattled, but I knew I had no choice.

"Hey," I said when Matt picked up the phone.

"Hey! I'm so glad you called. I was making the Chex…"

I interrupted. "I'm really sorry, but I won't be able to help you study this weekend," I said, trying to hide my devastation. "I'm not really feeling well, and I need to go to the doctor." I would not dare tell Matt the true reason for calling off our date, afraid of how he would react, or the rumors that would spread.

"You seemed fine at school today," Matt said, questioning my excuse.

"Yeah, I just…it just came out of nowhere. I'm sorry," I blurted out and quickly hung up the phone.

Fortunately, Mom had missed only a few days of pills, so Doctor Lantire was able to bring her blood levels back to normal rather quickly with a mix of lithium and quetiapine. Mom was well enough by the following week, and we were able to sleep in our own beds a few days later. Matt, who considered my cancellation as rejection, never spoke to me again.

~

I didn't give up on dating however, and my first steady relationship started almost a year later right before I turned sixteen. I was now a sophomore in high school, and Oliver who lived in a town close to Nutley, was a junior. He had light freckled skin, wavy blond hair, and to me, seemed mature, probably because of how tall he was. Brianne, a good friend of mine who I started talking to in middle school, introduced us.

One afternoon in October of 1998, Brianne, Victor, and I were sitting on the front porch of Victor's mother's duplex. Victor was telling me how he wanted to introduce me to a friend of his. Right on cue, a car came racing down the street and out the window of the beat-up silver sedan, I heard, "I want her!" as it flew by. I immediately felt lucky that someone older and ever so bold would want to be with me.

Oliver parked at his house down the street and came strutting back to us, cigarette smoke wafting from his fingertips. When he reached the stoop, he put his arm around me and smiled as he messed up my hair a bit.

"Hi, I'm Oliver," he said with confidence as I blushed.

"I'm Michelle."

Oliver and I started dating from that moment on and spent a lot of our time together at his house with his mother, who, much like my mother, seemed to be more of the lax parenting type, letting her son get away with quite a bit. During our time together, Oliver spent time with my mother almost every week, and Dad, only once. Mom treated him well and greeted him with a smile every time he came to the house. I think she was just excited for me to have my first real boyfriend. Oliver seemed to get along with her too and would always ask if she could join us out at dinner or on our dates. On the other hand, my father and Jillian were busy with my new sister, who was about to turn one. Bringing Oliver to Dad's house seemed more stressful than anything, and I preferred to stay away. Though I do remember my father and Oliver bonding over old cars.

Oliver and I spent most weekends together, except for the days when he said he had plans. I had a sinking feeling he was lying, but I couldn't pinpoint why. I think it had to do with the way he would cancel our plans at the last minute, saying he'd like to meet up with his friends instead. The only friend I ever met of his was Victor though, and he was always with Brianne. I couldn't prove that he was cheating and figured it must be in my head. Plus, I liked hanging out with him, and the way he made me feel when we were together, so I tried not to question it.

Around the one-month mark, Oliver sat me down on his bed in the attic. It was a large room, at least from what I remember—everything always seemed much larger then than they do now. The room was almost always a mess. Dishes and old clothes were strewn about the floor and the bed was usually unmade. It was private though, so we spent quite a bit of time up there.

"I think it's time we talk about having sex," he said.

I was taken aback by the comment and honestly, a little confused. I had never even mentioned that to him. "Oh, I didn't know you were thinking about that with me," I said. "You know, I've never done that before. I don't think I'm ready yet."

"It's not really a big deal," Oliver said. "I promise. I've done it before, and I'll go slow with you."

"Oh, well, I'm still not sure." I pulled away.

He looked at me. "Well, if you don't want to, I think we should just break up then. I mean, what's the point of being together if I can't be close to you?"

And with that, rather than feeling angry, I felt sad. I didn't have many other people in my life, and I didn't want to lose him. So, I questioned myself. *Was it really a big deal anyway?*

"I mean I guess we could try if you want." I thought back to the moment at Oak Beach with Ian. It seemed like this was the way boys were supposed to treat girls.

The next night, I walked into the room—I was pleasantly surprised to find it had been tidied and looked clean. Oliver spread roses on his bed and turned the lights low. He put an R&B CD into the player and turned the volume up so his mother wouldn't hear the two of us. In the center, Oliver stood with a wide grin on his face. Thinking back to his expression now, I should have slapped it, but as a sixteen-year-old girl, I thought it was sweet.

"The bed looks so pretty," I said. "Thank you." I was incredibly nervous, but the feeling lifted after seeing the array of petals.

The two of us began to kiss and Oliver laid me down on the bed. He removed my pants, and I apprehensively took off my shirt. As soon as it started though, I pushed back.

"This really hurts," I said.

"It's fine. You have to give it a few minutes."

"I don't like it."

What followed is difficult to describe with certainty, because at the time, I wasn't sure how to assert myself clearly. From my perspective, I don't remember Oliver stopping or doing it slowly like he had promised the day before. The only thing I recall was him pausing after he noticed the distressed expression on my face. It was probably only five minutes into it, though it felt like an hour, and he asked if it was okay to keep going, reminding me yet again that it would start to feel better soon.

"I don't know. I guess," I said.

After another painful few minutes, it ended. I sat up as Oliver put his arm around my shoulders and kissed me.

"I thought that was really nice," Oliver said.

"Yeah," I said just to say something.

Then, I not only questioned myself, but I also questioned everything about that moment. *Was this how I was supposed to experience my first time? Did I do it too soon? Was it supposed to hurt like that?* I heard from Brianne that it would be unpleasant, but this was something different. It wasn't just painful—I felt…sad.

"Next time it'll feel better," he said.

"I hope so."

Our relationship lasted another three months, at which point I discovered he had been cheating on me with not one, but a few other girls. Brianne, and two other friends of mine, Kathleen and Isabelle, asked me to meet up with them after school one day.

I entered Kathleen's bedroom, and it was as if I were walking into an intervention of some sort. I noticed the expressions on their faces and knew they were going to tell me something I didn't want to hear.

"Michelle, there's something we need to tell you," Kathleen said, as I sat next to her on the bed covered in faces of Derek Jeter. We were still such kids.

"What's going on?" I asked.

"We saw Oliver kissing another girl last week," Brianne said. "I'm so sorry." Isabelle sat silently, not knowing what to say.

"What?" My stomach dropped. "Who?"

"We don't know. Victor didn't want me to say anything, but I couldn't keep this from you," Brianne said. "You're our friend."

I was dumbfounded, completely taken off guard. What's worse though, is that I didn't believe them. I *couldn't* believe them. *How could I let something like this happen to me? Wasn't I smarter than this?* My friends put their arms around me and I cried. But then, after thinking to myself for a few minutes, I got up to leave the room.

"Where are you going?" Kathleen asked.

"I have to talk to Oliver," I said.

"He's not going to admit it," she said before I walked out.

She was right. Oliver denied any cheating and was able to hold that lie for the next two weeks until he finally admitted he had been seeing someone else. I was heartbroken. At only sixteen years old, my sense of trust in men had eroded to almost nothing.

Chapter 10
When I Left Myself

September 2000

Two years passed since Oliver and I broke up and, during that time, I found myself coming out of my shell a bit more. I was about to turn eighteen, and as a senior in high school, I started drinking and going to parties, finding that I could let others into my life, albeit slowly. I was also eager to apply to college, to get away from Nutley and the troubles I faced at home.

Over the past couple years, my relationship with my father grew even more distant as I started doing my own thing and making my own plans. Jillian was now pregnant with their second, who we later found out was another girl, and she and my father were focused on that and their daughter. I knew my father and Jillian wanted me there, but at this point in my life, I wanted to hang out with my boyfriend or my friends on the weekends rather than spend it with children.

If I had to choose between the two, I would have rather spent my weekends at home with Mom. I felt awkward around Jillian for no reason other than she was quiet and I liked being my outspoken self, something I couldn't really do at my father's. Plus, Mom often let me get away with spending more time out of the house than my father, giving me more freedom in my choices. This is not to say my life at Mom's was perfect, and there was frequent tension.

For one, Mom continued to experience regular bipolar symptoms, although it was controlled to an extent with medication. During her deeply depressive states, she would withdraw from the world, while her manic episodes, though less common and never as intense as they were when I was a child, brought their own disorder to our increasingly chaotic world. I couldn't comprehend the depth of her illness, nor could I truly empathize with what my mother was going through, and although I tried my best to avoid conflict, I had no control over her emotions. Her anxiety, depression, and anger were unyielding, and after years of swallowing my own emotions in silence, I started to reciprocate, causing issues in our relationship.

Secondly, our financial situation had gone from worse to dismal and I'd been frustrated that Mom was calling out of work at least once a week for a month or two. She was working part-time at a pet supply company as a receptionist but required to go in five days a week. I knew she didn't love her job, but if Mom got fired, she'd have to file for bankruptcy. This, we all knew, would mean losing the house right away. Selling the house was inevitable, but we all wanted to wait until at least Sam started college.

For the past eight years since the divorce, Dad paid the mortgage on our house. He had told me he knew Mom's salary was not sufficient and didn't want me and Sam to be forced to move. He also paid child support and alimony, which helped pay some of Mom's bills, but since she had difficulty finding, much less keeping, a job with her illness, whatever my father provided was the large majority of the money supporting us.

As soon as Mom felt secure that she was earning a steady working income, something would occur that would set her off. When this happened, she would call out of work for several days in a row, or if the depression lingered, she would have to be hospitalized and miss weeks on end. She was let go from her first job when the divorce papers were signed, her second when Dad proposed to Jillian, and her third when her mother was diagnosed with dementia, all within the span of four years. Years later, as I write this, I understand that this was not through any fault of her own, but because of the power the illness had over her mind and body. Back then though, I was not only scared, but livid.

Mom applied for government assistance, but it was barely enough to pay the remaining household expenses, which popped up often due to the old age of the house. Sam and I often lived on packaged food, like bread and pasta, when we weren't at Dad's house, which was most of the time. At home, the fridge was often bare, containing the occasional carton of eggs and a bottle of soda or milk. Mom couldn't afford much else.

My mother wanted to work, and she did, but she didn't have the experience, education, nor mental capacity to maintain a high paying, full-time salaried job. Sam and I didn't expect a thing for Christmas or our birthdays, and we accepted it—almost welcomed it—knowing she couldn't afford much and preferring she not spend the money.

With little money to spend, and most of Dad's child support covering living expenses, I got my first job as a cashier at a small local convenience store right before I entered high school. It was a simple job, as I stood behind the lone cash register waiting for the occasional customer to come strolling in. Every now and then, someone would come into the store and take out a small bag filled with coins to pay for whatever they put onto the conveyor belt. Knowing how my own mother had struggled financially, I recognized the same worry in these customers' eyes and would let them take their groceries even if they were a few dollars short. After a few months, I was, of course, fired.

I couldn't go very long without earning any money though if I wanted to buy clothes or anything for myself really, so I applied to a larger grocery store chain, and they hired me as a cashier a week later. With that, along with a few babysitting jobs, I was able to save up enough to buy a car with some help from my father.

On the relationship front, I was now with Trevor, who I first was introduced to not long before I started dating Oliver. I was seeing one of Trevor's friends, Nick, who I met while I was working at the grocery chain. Nick was blunt and outspoken, one of those guys who could talk to anyone, but also one who didn't seem to care what others thought. Trevor and Nick had been close friends since they were kids, but Trevor's view of him steadily changed when he noticed how he treated me—at least that's what Trevor had once told me. Nick and I only dated for a month, yet after we broke up, Trevor and I remained friends, hanging out after school and shopping at the mall on the weekends. That is, until I met Oliver, and our friendship faded. We rarely spoke during my first two years of high school but then reconnected during junior year. Trevor declared his feelings for me, and I was ecstatic, feeling the same for Trevor, but never able to admit it before then.

Trevor wasn't like my previous boyfriends—he was kind. He truly seemed to care about my feelings, and what I wanted; I felt safe around him.

I was relatively tall for my age, but Trevor towered over me at 6'2". He was a basketball player at a nearby private high school, and his stature could have easily intimidated anyone. But behind that strong exterior, he had a sweetness few ever saw, and I found myself strongly attracted to it. He had deep hazel eyes, a shaved head, and we shared a unique sense of humor that only the two of us could understand.

It was fall of 2000, and Trevor and I had been dating for a year. Things were going well in our relationship, and the love we shared for each other was almost perfect, so much so that, at eighteen, I already envisioned spending the rest of my life with him. We talked endlessly about marriage, children, and growing old together as I imagined the life I always wanted for myself but never had.

I had just walked home from school one afternoon, and was excited to call Trevor, like I did every day, but stopped first in the kitchen to grab a snack. There, I saw Mom sitting at the table with her checkbook open to pay bills.

"How was your day at school?" Mom asked.

"Good," I replied simply, grabbing a liter of soda from the fridge.

"Don't drink that crap. It's full of sugar," Mom pressed, watching me chug the soda straight from the bottle. Everything was a battle, even the small things.

"It's fine, Mom." I was frustrated that she would have the nerve to tell me how to act. After eight years of running the household, I felt like I should be making my own decisions.

"No, it's not. Put it away!" Mom raised her voice

"Don't tell me what to do," I retorted with my voice also now raised.

"Michelle, I am your mother!"

"Then act like it sometimes!" I snapped, remembering yet another incident from a week before when Mom had completely forgotten to pick Sam up from school. I would have walked home with Sam myself, but I had to babysit, and really, it was the principle of the matter that angered me.

"How dare you talk to me like that!" Mom screamed with a sharp bitterness to her tone, almost as if a witch was stirring her cauldron.

"Oh, please!" I shouted back as I ran up to my room and slammed the door shut.

"You are exactly like your father!" Mom yelled after me with the same coldness in her voice. She would often say this, but I never knew exactly how to take it. From my mother's tone, I could tell it was meant as an insult, yet even after all these years, she still loved my father. *So, did that mean this was the only way she knew how to show love for me? Or did she hate me because of what she was going through with him?* I couldn't figure it out and it was getting to the point where I had to simply ignore her comments because they were too painful to hear.

My heart pounding from anxiety, I dragged my wired pink neon phone to the bed, about to dial Trevor's house. Before I could, though, I looked up to see Sam standing in my doorway.

She seemed crushed and must have heard my fight with Mom from her bedroom.

"It's my fault Mommy is like this. It's all my fault," Sam cried, tears flowing down her face. "If I didn't get sick, none of this would have happened. She would have been happy."

Without hesitation, I rushed over to Sam and wrapped my arms around her slim body. "You never ever think that way again," I said firmly yet calmly. "This is not your fault. This is no one's fault." I refused to let Sam break. My little sister, who was now a freshman in high school and not so little anymore, was the glue that kept me from breaking.

"I know. I just wish Mommy would go back to normal. Like how she was when we were kids before Daddy moved out."

"Me too, Sam," I commiserated. "Me too." I looked Sam in the eyes and said, "We'll get through this. We always do."

"You're right," Sam said, wiping a tear away. She paused before speaking again. "Is Trevor coming over tonight?"

"I'm not sure. I'm about to call him."

"Oh, I really hope he does. He always makes me laugh," Sam said. "Plus, he makes you so happy!"

"He really does."

"But hey, I have to get to work. Sorry to run out on you, but thanks for listening to me. I'll see you later." Sam rushed out the door, her eyes still red from tears.

I took a moment before picking up the phone.

"Hey, honey," Trevor answered. He must have seen the caller ID.

"I can't be in this house. I just can't," I complained.

"What happened this time?"

"She's just impossible to live with. Everything I do or say, I get yelled at," I started rambling. "Plus, I'm starting to see how Sam is affected. And on top of everything, I have my AP bio exam next week and I don't think I'm ready."

"You've been studying for weeks. You'll do well." Trevor reassured me. The phone was silent for a few seconds, and then he continued. "Listen, your mother has issues, at least from what you tell me, but you're still her daughter. Maybe you shouldn't be so harsh."

Why is that an excuse? I thought. Then I asked Trevor, "She's the adult. Shouldn't she be the one to stop yelling? She picks fights with me all the time."

"I get it," Trevor said. "And I'm sorry."

"It's okay." I let out a slow, defeated exhale. "Thanks for letting me vent."

"Hey, tonight, the guys and I are getting together at eight. Why don't you come with us?"

"Yeah, I will. The usual spot?" I knew the abandoned garage well.

"Yep," Trevor said. "Listen, it'll be good for you to get out of the house. We'll have a good time tonight."

"I hope you're right."

"I know I'm right," Trevor said. "I love you!"

"Love you too." I hung up the phone, feeling more relaxed than I had a few minutes earlier.

A moment later, there was a tap on the door. "Can I come in?" Mom asked timidly. The anger from before seemingly disappeared from her expression, and mine started to return.

"Sure," I said in a sharp tone.

"I'm sorry for yelling before. I know it can be difficult when I get like that," she said calmly. "I want to explain something to you. Sam's a little too young, but I think maybe you'd understand."

"Okay?" I was now attentive. Normally I'd brush her off, shying away from any emotional moment like this, but there was something about her tone that made me want to talk to her. I shoved my biology book off to the side as Mom took a seat next to me.

"I know I get mad and yell sometimes. I hate the medicine I've been given and it makes me feel like I'm floating half the time. Sometimes my brain feels so foggy and I get confused easily. That can be frustrating, and I take it out on you. I'm sorry," she apologized, and then continued. "But when I'm off the medicine, it's much worse. My depression...it feels like I'm being...sucked into a blackhole, but all I..." Mom took a pause. "...all I can do is fight with every ounce of my strength to remain free. It's unbearable and I can't help it."

"Mom, it's okay," I said softly. "What's it like? The disease..." I stopped.

"Go ahead sweetie," Mom said in a comforting tone.

"Will I get it?"

"I don't think so honey. In my situation, something very serious caused my illness to activate. I don't think anything like that will happen to you."

What she said did not ease my concerns though. *How was my mother to predict the future? How was she to know nothing serious would happen?* I could have kept going with her, asking more questions, but I didn't and let it go. "Okay. I'm sorry you feel this way and I'm sorry I get short with you too," I said. "I'll try to be more understanding." She gave me a hug, and then, deep in the awkward emotional moment, I lightened it up with a joke. "Maybe we could just run off to a secret tropical island. You'd never be sad there, right?"

"Oh, I wish we could, sweetie!"

"Me too. Hey, Trevor invited me out tonight with the guys. I'll stay for dinner but then I gotta head out."

"Why don't you invite Trev here for dinner and you can head out together?"

"Great idea. Thanks Mom," I said with a smile.

That night, Mom hurried about the kitchen preparing my favorite meal, while Sam, Trevor, and I sat patiently waiting for Mom to bring the food to the dining room table. Sam took a liking to Trevor the day she met him. As a young teenager, she was shy meeting my boyfriends, always saying "hi", but then running off to her room to play or do homework. But when Trevor showed up at the house and gave her a big hug as soon as he walked through the door, he bypassed the tension, and Sam opened up to him more than I'd seen her do with anyone else.

Mom pushed through the swinging pantry doors with a bright smile on her face, one that I hadn't seen in a long time. She was holding a tray of steaming lasagna and placed it in the center of the table. We all dove in. Mom, like Sam, fell in love with Trevor almost immediately and treated him like a son, much like Oliver. However, Trevor was day, while Oliver was night.

"So, where are you two headed tonight?" Mom asked.

"They'll probably get drunk again," Sam chimed in.

"Sam, come on," I said, trying to shush her.

"What? You always do. It's no secret," Sam said. She was not letting up.

"I know it's not a secret. Mom knows," I said. "I'd just rather her find out after the fact."

"I do know. Just don't turn into a lush," Mom said.

"So, Sam, do you like your new job at the ice cream store?" Trevor asked, changing the subject.

"Yeah, but my arm is killing me," Sam grimaced and then pulled up her sleeve to expose her arm to everyone.

"Oh Sam! That arm is twice the size of your other," Mom said. "I'm going to make a doctor's appointment first thing tomorrow."

"It's fine. I just whacked it while I was scooping ice cream last week," Sam explained.

"That's not a bruise, Sam. You need to get that checked," I said, concerned.

"Whatever, sure. I will," Sam conceded. It was obvious Sam didn't like it when I took control of something she should be responsible for. We were a lot alike.

"Promise me?" I asked.

"Yes, I promise."

Trevor finished eating and after I took my last bite, he picked up both of our dishes and brought them to the kitchen. I noticed the way Mom smiled at him, as if he were doing something right. When he returned, I stood up from my chair before Trevor had a chance to sit back down.

"Hey, we have to head out," I said. "The guys are waiting."

"Already? Trevor just got here," Mom said, disappointed.

"I know, I'm sorry. I'll see you later! Love you!" I pushed Trevor out the front door before Mom could pull us back.

"Love you!" Trevor yelled back at Mom.

"Love you both," Mom shouted after us. "Be careful!"

As we held hands walking to the car, Trevor kissed me play-fully.

"I missed you! I haven't seen you all week," he said happily.

I kissed him back. "Who's coming tonight?" I loved hanging out with Trevor's friends. They were easy going and fun to be with, most of them at least.

"Aaron and Dom."

"Ugh, all Aaron does is smoke weed," I complained.

"Oh, I was hoping you wouldn't say that. I was thinking maybe we could smoke with them tonight."

"You and me?"

"Yeah, why not?" Trevor questioned. "I'll be with you."

"Umm yeah I guess," I said hesitantly. I didn't love the idea of trying something that could mess with my mind, especially after what I witnessed my mother go through. I drank alcohol, but drugs, they seemed different to me, more mentally aggravating. Plus, bipolar disorder ran in the family. *Could drugs be the thing to "activate my illness", as Mom mentioned earlier?*

I knew Trevor would never force me into doing something I didn't want to do, something I appreciated quite a bit, but I still felt a sense of pressure. I didn't love it when Trevor drank or smoked without me. He would often drink a few too many beers and then I'd be responsible for taking care of him, yet another person in my life. Or he'd smoke too much weed and just sit in a corner laughing to himself all night.

Trevor turned into the empty lot and parked under the single yellow streetlight. We got out of the car and opened the door into the expansive garage furnished only with a small portable fridge, a folding table, and four beach chairs that sat next to a rugged, beat-up couch. We walked up to Aaron and Dom who were already there waiting for us.

"Hey, guys," Aaron shouted. "I got the good stuff tonight!"

"Hey, Michelle," Dom said. "I haven't seen you in a while. I've missed you!"

"I've missed you too!" I ran over to give him a big hug. Next to him was Aaron, who sat on the couch and was bent over the table filling a large bong.

"Trev, we're smoking out of that?" I asked anxiously.

"Yeah, just start with a small hit," Trevor said. "You'll be okay. And again, if you don't want to do it, you don't have to."

Aaron covered the opening of the bong, which must have been at least a foot tall, with his mouth, and lit the bowl packed with weed. As he took the first hit, smoke filled the base and quickly traveled up to his mouth. His hit was long and deep, and he coughed a few times, but then he sat back in his seat and relaxed.

Dom took a hit next, and then it was Trevor's turn. After Trevor took his hit, he gave me a look that said, "you don't have to do this." It was as if he just realized the drug's potency.

But I wasn't about to back down. I sat next to Trevor and took a hit, small at first, but then Aaron encouraged me to take more. "Come on, Michelle, hit it like you mean it! You won't feel anything after that baby hit."

Trevor put his hand on my shoulder to stop me, but I shrugged him off. Maybe I had something to prove to Aaron, or maybe to myself. Maybe I had to prove that I could handle whatever was thrown at me even if I was scared. I stared at Aaron as I sucked up the cloud of smoke in a single gulp.

I sat back and waited, not knowing what to expect. It took a minute, but then I noticed my thinking was off. Trevor said something rather random, probably funny, about a chipmunk, and I started laughing hysterically for what felt like a very long minute. The laughter wasn't joyful though—it was almost manic, and that terrified me. Moments later, when I came down from my high, I felt disoriented. I didn't like the sensation at all. But then I was off again, laughing uncontrollably at something else completely mundane. The second time I returned to myself, I looked at Trevor.

"Trev, I don't like this," I said. "I want to go home." This feeling of not being myself, not having control over my thoughts, frightened me. *Is this how Mom felt? Is this what her mania was like? Am I going to get sick?* The thoughts ran rampant and I couldn't stop them, nor could I make sense of them.

"Okay, well, uh…hey listen. I can't really drive right now," he said. "Can you give me a little time?"

"I'm not feeling right. I want to go."

"Hey Aaron, can you drive?" Trevor asked.

"Yeah, I'm good," Aaron confirmed. "Why, what's up?"

"I think Michelle needs to get home," Trevor said. "Now."

"Oh. Oh yeah, I gotcha. Michelle, you okay?" Aaron asked concerned.

"Yeah," I said, even though I wasn't.

"This stuff is really strong," Dom said.

"Yeah, the weed I usually get from this guy is good, but this is out there," Aaron said and started to giggle.

"Okay, let's get in the car," Trevor said, encouraging them to get up and go.

The four of us piled into Aaron's black Honda Accord, and as I lay curled up in Trevor's lap in the backseat, I remember Aaron telling us on repeat that someone in his family was a prominent police officer in town and that he believed he could get out of any ticket. Unfortunately, what this also meant was that he did not care about his speed, or really his driving for that matter, and he flew down the side streets, passing through yellow-turned-red lights with Eminem blasting at full volume. I clutched onto Trevor's leg hoping that somehow his upper thigh would save me if we did actually crash. The drive seemed painfully long, but somehow, we arrived safely.

"Trev, when I can drive, I'll bring your car back here and Aaron can drive me home," Dom offered as Trevor and I stepped out of the car.

"Thanks man," Trevor said.

Trevor and I walked up the first flight of steps to the front yard, which was situated high off the sidewalk. My anxiety was building by this time, and I hated how my brain was working. I just wanted to get into bed and go to sleep.

Mom opened the front door.

"Is everything okay?" she asked.

"Michelle needs to get to bed," Trevor said.

At that moment, Mom rushed down from the front porch in a panic and looked into my eyes as I stared at her blankly. "What did she take?" Mom looked at Trevor. She seemed nervous.

"We just smoked weed. It was strong, and this was her first time," Trevor explained.

"Oh boy," Mom said, sounding relieved, probably because I didn't do ecstasy or heroin or something like that. "Okay, let's get her to her room."

With Trevor's help, I walked slowly up the set of cement stairs to the front door. Then, leaning into Trevor, I trudged up the next set of stairs to my room. I settled into bed fully clothed, and Mom covered me with the comforter after she removed my sneakers.

And then it happened. I started panicking in a way I had never felt before, shaking uncontrollably and feeling like I couldn't catch my breath.

"Mom," I said. "I feel like I'm outside my body. I don't know what's happening to me." This sense of detachment, the feeling of floating above and looking down over my physical self—it seemed to me way worse than anything my mother had experienced in the more than twelve years since she'd been diagnosed with bipolar disorder. I did not just feel like I was high—I felt like I had died.

Years later, I would come to learn that what I had experienced was a dissociative panic attack. As I write this, it has been twenty-five years since the incident, and I can still recall it like it was yesterday. The feeling of separation, literal disconnection from my body was an utterly terrifying, yet oddly freeing, detachment from reality. I looked at my hands, but they were not *my* hands; I looked at my arms, but they were not *my* arms. My mind was literally "checking out", one, because I was high, and two, because I was having a panic attack. No matter how hard I tried, I could not re-associate with myself; I could not *become* myself. I knew something bad was happening, and although my mind was racing, I could not grab onto any of my thoughts. They all seemed fleeting, running away from me as if I had been desperately chasing them.

"It's okay, sweetie," Mom said soothingly. I heard her, but she sounded muffled. She looked at Trevor. "Was the weed laced with anything?"

"I don't think so. I mean, I smoked it," Trevor said. "It's strong for sure but I don't think anything else was in it. Dom and Aaron are okay too."

"I see." It took a few seconds but then Mom sat on my bed, looked at me with a seriousness she rarely exhibited and said, "Michelle, you fight this. You fight this with all your life." It was as if she knew this was more than just the drugs.

Although the thoughts in my mind were scrambled, I recalled the conversation with her earlier in the night and wholeheartedly understood. And even though I knew what she was trying to tell me, I felt like I had already messed up. In one single hour, it felt like I had changed my destiny. The drugs activated the illness, and there was nothing I could do—I was doomed to the same fate as my mother.

Trevor gave me a kiss on his way out, and as he opened the bedroom door to leave, Max came running in and jumped up on my bed, curling up in between my legs. My fifteen-pound dog was a source of comfort that no human could provide. My body started to calm, and I finally drifted off to sleep.

The next morning, I woke up to my mother lying next to me, and I felt better. The path I had prematurely determined for myself nine hours earlier in my panicked state was slowly taking on a new shape. I felt off, a little hazy and spaced out, but I had somehow grounded myself in my sleep. I felt like myself again and breathed a heavy sigh of relief. Mental illness was not on my so-called horizon, at least not yet.

Sam strolled into my room. "Mom, did you sleep with Michelle?" She was confused as she brushed past the stick figures drawn on the wall and pulled a shirt from my closet without asking.

"Yeah, she wasn't feeling great last night," Mom told her as I remained beside her, awake.

"Oh, is she okay?"

"I'm fine. I'm still a little off, but feeling better," I cut in and then turned to Mom. "Thanks for staying with me all night. I think I'm done with weed for a while."

"Good idea, kiddo," Mom said. "I love you."

"Wait, *you* smoked weed?" Sam asked shocked.

"Unfortunately, yeah," I said. "Not a fan."

"Hey, Sam, I'm gonna call the doctor soon," Mom interrupted. "I'll try to get you in today."

"Mom, I'm fine I swear," Sam said.

"Sam, you really need to go. Your arm is huge," I urged, agreeing with Mom. "Plus, you promised me."

"Fine…just let me know what time," Sam said, relenting.

That afternoon, Sam went to the doctor and next thing I knew, I was visiting her at Stonewall Hospital.

~

"I told you so!" I joked as I entered her hospital room. Mom and Dad were both there, not speaking to each other, but remaining surprisingly civil.

"Michelle! This is serious," Mom exclaimed.

"I know, I'm sorry. Are you okay?"

"Yeah. They say the blood clot should clear up with blood thinners over the next few weeks. I just need to take it easy," Sam explained. "Oh, and quit my job."

"That makes sense. You can't scoop ice cream all day with that thing," I said. "But you know what you can do?"

"What?"

"You can help me babysit that little brat. You know, the annoying Pinter kid I watch sometimes?" I joked.

"I'll pass, thanks," Sam said, smiling.

"Sam, how are you feeling?" Dad asked.

"I'm fine. I didn't feel anything really," Sam said. "I just have a left arm the size of a blimp now."

"Oh, I really hadn't noticed," Dad teased. Her arm was obviously much larger than the other. "The doctor said it should go back to its normal size over time."

"I hope so," Sam said.

"Alright, listen, I have to get out of here. It was good seeing you girls," Dad said, never acknowledging Mom. "I'll see you tomorrow." He kissed Sam on the forehead and whispered something in her ear.

"Bye, Dad," Sam and I said in unison as he left the room.

"He's a ball of laughs, right girls?" Mom said, trying to get a smile out of either of us. But at the end of the day, he was still my father.

"Mom, stop," I said, waving off the insult. Mom rolled her eyes as I continued to ignore her. "I'm going to run to the vending machine."

And I walked out of the room.

C h a p t e r   11

Learning to Carry It

November 2000

Over the next few weeks, Sam recovered, but my mother—she started to spiral out of control. Sam's episode, the approaching holidays, something triggered my mother, and she couldn't stop talking about when Sam was sick years ago. Days turned into weeks, and Mom stopped taking her medication, once again falling into a deep depression. She called out of work for an entire week and, as I later found out, she was let go from her job. When she wouldn't respond to me using more than a single word, I knew something was seriously wrong.

I was aware, of course, that Mom had been admitted to the hospital before, but this was the first time I was old enough to decide for myself whether she should go or not. Still, the choice wasn't clear.

It was late afternoon one Sunday, and I had just returned home from babysitting. I phoned Aunt Gail from the kitchen and kept my voice low so that my mother could not hear me.

"Hello?" Gail answered.

"Hi, Aunt Gail."

"Michelle? Everything okay?" Gail's voice was laced with concern.

"I'm not sure. I think my mom needs to go to the hospital."

"No, please don't say that," Gail replied. "Tell me what happened."

"I'm pretty sure she stopped taking her medication again. She's sitting on the couch watching some game show, but she looks almost catatonic."

"Don't bring her back to the hospital," Gail said forcefully. "We can figure something out."

"Well, what am I supposed to do?" I felt both confused and frustrated.

"Get her to take the medication she already has. I'm sure there's enough for her," my aunt said. "I'd hate it if she went to that place again. Wouldn't you? You don't want her there, right?" She knew how to lay it on thick.

Of course I didn't want her there, but I didn't know what else to do. I argued, "Aunt Gail, she's not safe here. She could walk out, or fall, or even turn the stove on and walk away. I can't stay home from school all week to keep an eye on her."

"You're her daughter. You can figure it out," Gail said, then hung up.

I was infuriated. I waited for Sam to return from the mall with her friends.

"Hey Sam, can you come here?" I called when I heard the front door open. After a minute, she stepped into the kitchen and closed the door.

"I saw Mommy on the couch. Is she okay?" At fourteen, Sam was old enough to understand when Mom wasn't well.

"I think she needs to go to the hospital. I called Aunt Gail, but after talking to her, all I feel is guilty. We have no other option though," I said, still in a low voice. "I don't know who else to turn to. I think we should take her ourselves."

"Yes, you're right."

"I'll drive," I said. "Can you come with me?"

"Yes, of course."

We led Mom out the back door to the driveway off the yard. When Mom was in this state of mind, she was compliant, though confused, and followed us like a ghost to the car without a word. That is, until she asked, "Where are we going?"

This right here was the question I was dreading. The question that, if I answered truthfully, would halt her compliance and lead to some sort of heavy emotion or physical protest. I had seen it more than once when I was a child and my father had to physically carry her out of the house, or more recently when my aunt or uncle got involved. It was something I knew Sam and I could not handle ourselves.

"The ice cream store," I lied.

Despite the ever-growing guilt that washed over me, Sam and I drove her to the psychiatric unit at Stonewall Hospital. When the hospital came into view, and my lie exposed, my mother instantly objected, screaming incoherently and cursing angrily at us for the decision we made. We were forced to ignore her, as a mother may endure a child's meltdown. In order to get her out of the car, we had to drive up to the front entrance and ask medical staff to help us. There, they removed her from her seat and carried her to the unit, as we followed with our heads down low.

The psychiatric unit housed about twenty patients at a time. Mom was given a shared room with another patient who slept most of the day and night, except for the times when she jolted herself awake with her own snoring. The room was bland and white, with a simple curtain separating the two beds; it reminded me of a very similar hospital room we had become accustomed to many years earlier when Sam was a baby.

Sam and I helped Mom settle into her space and told the nurse we would be back later with extra clothes and toiletries. What happened next was something I probably should have expected, but didn't, and it blindsided me in a way I never anticipated.

After we said our goodbyes, Mom didn't remain in her room; rather, she followed us. She was oddly quiet though and walked behind us to the double doors that were locked from the inside, as if she were going to leave with us. A nurse was close behind her, seemingly waiting for some inevitable scenario to occur. As soon as the staff unlocked the doors, the nurse grabbed my mother's arm in a tight hold, and, as if the gates of Hell had just opened, Mom began to wail, begging for us not to leave.

Sam and I turned around, stunned by the scene that was unfolding in front of us. I had no idea what to do. I looked to the nurse, who, with a gentle expression on her face, told us to leave and not look back. We listened to her and walked out the door as Mom's sobs burned a hole right through my heart.

Mom remained hospitalized for ten days. I had just turned eighteen, so I was perfectly capable of caring for Sam and myself, and Mom being out of the house for a few days wasn't difficult. I made sure Sam went to school each day, though it's not like I needed to remind her, and I used my own money to buy food and other essentials.

While in the hospital, Mom continually improved each day with the prescribed medication. After a week, the doctors and I agreed that she could come home before Christmas, and we made plans to pick her up over the next few days.

Upon returning home, Mom was slightly incoherent, but she eventually returned to herself. It seemed the combination of both Sam being in the hospital and the upcoming holidays were what set her off because soon after Christmas, Mom was back to normal. On Christmas Day itself, Sam and I endured the usual stress of trying to keep Mom happy as we opened the few presents we were able to afford, but other than that, it was relatively uneventful, though still festive.

It was now January 2001, and I had returned to my senior year of high school after the break.

"I have some good news," Mom declared one evening after I arrived home from school.

"Oh yeah?" I replied, plopping my backpack down on the now dark evergreen living room carpet. After the divorce, Mom changed the color of the carpet, though as I write this now, I have no idea where she got the money to do so.

"I got a new job!" Mom exclaimed.

"What are you talking about? You have a job?" I was unaware that she had lost her previous position. I wasn't excited like she was; I was concerned and frustrated.

"It just wasn't working out. I hated being a receptionist anyway," she said, talking faster, the words tumbling out of her mouth. "I'll be working for a catering hall as a waitress. I'll meet so many new people, and the boss is great and…"

I cut her off. "And what are we going to do when we don't have enough money to buy food again?" I asked, assuming she'd eventually lose this job too.

"This time it will be different." Mom's voice softened.

"Whatever you say," I said, more irritated than comforted. I picked my backpack up off the ground and went to my room.

It turned out Mom was right about this one, however. Her boss, unlike her previous managers, was amenable to her condition and allowed her to take time off when she needed to. He seemed to care about *her*, and not just the bottom line. We finally had a steady income, and more importantly, peace of mind that Mom wouldn't lose her job like she had so many times in the past.

Unfortunately, the pay was barely enough to cover gas and groceries for the month. Mom was making slightly more than minimum wage, just eight dollars an hour, to waitress for weddings and other events on the weekends. She left the house before dinner, always making sure to prepare a meal for me and Sam before she went, and didn't return home until three in the morning most nights. Tips were scarce and her paychecks small. Mom rarely called out and only did when necessary. She earned a few hundred dollars a month. The only splurge she could afford was her monthly fifteen-dollar nail appointment and even that wasn't always guaranteed.

Even though the child support money was essentially cut in half when I turned eighteen, Mom was able to bring in enough to cover most of her living expenses. Even still, her financial troubles continued. I tried my best to save what I earned, but often, as soon as my savings reached a respectable limit, Mom would need the money to pay for something in the house that needed to be fixed, be it the leaking kitchen faucet, or the broken washing machine. Sam and I spent many nights doing homework sitting in the bathtub because turning on the exhaust fan was the only source of heat in the house. At that age, I couldn't understand why the bills weren't being paid and the night my mother emptied my savings account without notice became my breaking point.

"Mom, do you know what happened to the money in my account?" I asked. "It shows a fifteen-dollar balance, and I had about eight hundred dollars in there last week." I was oddly hopeful that the money had been stolen by someone else.

"I needed it, Michelle. It was an emergency," Mom snapped. She was angry at *me* for asking such a silly question.

"Are you serious? That was my money. What were you thinking?" I pressed, my voice raised.

"I needed the money to fix the water heater. I didn't know what else to do," Mom said, defensive. "We need hot water."

"Maybe if you saved your money instead of wasting it on things we don't need, like cigarettes, you'd have enough for a water heater," I said scornfully.

"Don't talk to me like that!" Mom shouted, her voice deep. "I am your mother whether you like it or not!"

"You better pay me back," I sneered.

I ran off to my bedroom, knowing she wasn't going to pay me back, and counted down to the days when I would be free from this after I moved away to college.

I also knew that while most of the money coming in was spent on essentials, my mother would occasionally spend above her means on things we didn't truly need—a gold bracelet for me or new shoes for Sam. It infuriated me that no extra money was put into a savings account. *Why did I need to remind my mother of this—wasn't she supposed to be the adult of the household?* Looking back though, I can only now understand the urge to make us happy.

Alone in my room, I called Trevor. "She stole my money, Trev," I said abruptly as soon as he said hello.

"She stole your money?" Trevor asked in disbelief.

"Yes. She took hundreds of dollars directly from my account without asking." My voice was shaking.

"Do you think maybe she needed it?" Trevor asked calmly, trying his best to settle me down. But I was furious and couldn't understand why my boyfriend was trying to make excuses for her.

"What are you talking about? I needed that money," I pleaded. "How am I going to pay for gas?" Just then, Max jumped up onto my bed and curled up next to me. His comforting presence cut through my aggravation, and I found myself cooling off as I gave him a scratch behind his ear.

"You know what? I've got it. Don't worry," Trevor reassured me. His family had money, at least more than we did, and even though he would frequently offer to pay for me when we were out, I felt wrong accepting his offers. This time, I truly had no other choice.

"Thank you. I appreciate it," I conceded, forcing myself to breathe.

I could always rely on Trevor to bring me down from the emotional hill I had constructed for myself. I was so in love with him that anything he said would help settle my nerves. I could tell him anything. Well, almost anything.

As close as I was with Trevor, never once during our relationship did I speak of the incident at Oak Beach, and it came to a point where I had buried it so deep that I almost forgot it happened myself. It was one of those memories where if I didn't think of it, didn't process it, it would stay far away, hidden in some mental chest where only I had the key. But if it popped up in my mind, for any reason whatsoever, I would remember every detail, every touch, every feeling as if it were yesterday.

Not only that, but I also glossed over my unhealthy relationship with Oliver when Trevor would ask about past boyfriends. I simply stated, "We dated for a few months. It was not that serious," though I didn't believe that at all.

It was only when Trevor and I became sexually active that I fully grasped how both experiences affected me. Until then, I had remained detached, trying as best I could never to think about them. But when Trevor asked me "Is this okay?" in a calm, sweet voice before we had sex for the first time, it hit me like a punch to the gut that my experiences with both Ian and Oliver had crossed boundaries for me.

I kept my silence though, never revealing anything to Trevor. *I'd suppressed those memories for years, so why should I say something now?* When we first had sex though, something inside me triggered. It was as if I was reliving the trauma I associated with them all over again. The first, when it happened and now, as I finally started to understand it. *How had I not seen this before?*

I began to have nightmares, replaying the moments in my head each night. I started questioning my relationship with Trevor. *Could I trust him? What if he did the same thing to me?* I loved Trevor but in my anxious state, I couldn't help but question his motives.

The lingering thoughts occupied the back of my mind as if they had parked in the spot I had left for them.

My relationship with Trevor progressed for the next year, through high school graduation into freshman year of college. During the college application process, I suggested that we both apply to several schools but keep one on the side that we could try for together. Deep down, I knew if we attended different colleges our relationship would be over, and I couldn't bear to lose him. Other than Sam, Trevor had been my rock, my constant, and knowing that Sam would remain home while I was at college, I was scared. I was afraid of the unknown, and of not having someone I loved and trusted close by to keep me grounded.

All the colleges I applied to were at least an hour away from home and it became an emotional tug of war between putting my mother's interests first and choosing what was best for me. She wanted me close, I assume, for emotional support, and probably financial, but would never outright say it knowing she would not get it from me. There was no more parental responsibility on my part since Sam would be almost sixteen, and in my mind, old enough to care for herself. Plus, Mom had been doing well. Even still, I felt immense guilt for prioritizing my own needs above hers. But in the end, for my own sanity, I knew living at home was not an option.

After months of touring colleges, Trevor decided on Syracuse University, which was the one school we had both applied to. I was relieved by his choice but also needed to wait for my scholarship and financial aid letters before I could decide whether I could afford to go there myself.

Two weeks later, I received the FAFSA acceptance letters. With financial aid and student loans, I opted to attend Syracuse as well.

Dad and Jillian said their goodbyes the night before I left. We all stood by the front door as I gave Jillian a hug and bent down to my two young sisters. I told them they could visit me whenever they wanted and that I'd be back for Thanksgiving. Then, I looked up at my father.

"You'll do well, sweetheart," he said as he gave me a tight hug. He seemed proud more than anything.

I finished packing up a few things from my bedroom and the next morning, I threw the bag into my car, excited for a new adventure. I woke up early to spend an hour with Max, taking him for a long walk through the park. I knelt beside him and told him I'd see him over Thanksgiving break. Then I cried more than I had with my father as I kissed him and ruffled his ears. His wagging tail drooped down slowly as I walked away with my suitcase.

The four-hour drive up to Syracuse with my mother and Sam was uneventful, minus the wrong turn we made near Poughkeepsie. We quickly got back on track though and made our way to the campus.

When we arrived, I unpacked my suitcases in the dorm room I was given. My roommate had already gotten there and set up her area. Lynn was sweet, quiet, and kept to herself most of the time. We got along well.

"Sam, you better visit," I said as she and Mom were getting ready for the trip home.

"I'll be back next weekend," Sam joked, with tears in her eyes. "But seriously, I'm going to miss you."

"I'll miss you too," I said, giving her a hug.

My mother gave up trying to hide her tears. "Michelle, this is your time to shine." She looked at me and gave me a big hug. Then, they walked away.

As luck would have it, Trevor and I were assigned to the same dorm building. We each formed our own friendships, but being so close to the man I loved, it became difficult to form an independence of my own. I found myself spending most of my time with Trevor.

Not three weeks after we moved into our dorm rooms, I received a call from Mom. I was alone in my room, studying for some quiz, while my roommate and Trevor were in class.

"Michelle, sweetheart, do you have a few minutes to talk?" Mom asked timidly.

I could tell right away there was something wrong. "Oh no, what is it?" I asked, solemnly as I closed my textbook.

"It's Max."

Of all the scenarios that ran through my mind in that moment, never did I expect it to be about my dog, my sweet Max. My heart dropped—I knew what she was going to say.

"No," I whispered, my body frozen in shock.

"I'm so sorry. He passed away peacefully on the kitchen floor. Sam and I were with him until the end," Mom shared softly.

"Mom, what happened?" I begged, my voice cracking. "He was fine when I left a few weeks ago."

"He was getting old, sweetheart. He was probably very sick and we didn't know. Dogs tend to hide their pain," Mom explained, although I had no idea how she would know that.

"I have to go." I choked up as I hung up the phone. I collapsed into my pillow as my emotions came crashing over me like a tidal wave. I sobbed uncontrollably, yet strangely enough I didn't feel any pain—just hollow numbness.

As soon as Trevor returned from class, I pulled him into my arms and explained what happened. I had experienced loss before when my grandmother died, or when my hamster was sent off to a "farm" as a child, but this felt different. This was more intense, dark. Max was more than a dog, he was my comfort when I needed him, and back at home, that was more often than not.

A day or so later, after the initial shock dissipated, the guilt slowly crept in. Max was my dog, and I wasn't by his side when he left this world. I couldn't help but think he must have been so scared, wondering where I was. I leaned into the last memory I had of him when I said goodbye. It wasn't enough though because there it was—that deep unshakable depression in the pit of my stomach.

Max's death stuck with me for months. I withdrew from the world and all my newly formed friends and acquaintances. I had no interest in doing anything but study. I gave myself over to Trevor, who supported me, but since he never experienced loss before, he didn't truly understand what I was going through. I think back to those days, those weeks, when I felt the deep sadness of Max's passing and it echoes ever so clearly now after a more recent dog of mine crossed the rainbow bridge. The pain is real, the depression poignant, and it can be debilitating.

Trevor and I continued dating into sophomore year, but as the months went by, we started to grow apart. Max's death was the start of a shift in our relationship where Trevor wanted to continue partying, and where I needed a break. When Friday nights came, I preferred to stay in and watch movies or read a book, while Trevor wanted to drink and hang out with friends. I compromised often though, but to me, it seemed like Trevor never wanted to stay in. Because of the difference in our choices, we started to fight, and our relationship suffered.

"Why don't you just flirt with her right in front of me, Trev?" I said scornfully. We had been at the basement party for hours. Music pounded in the dark, and the keg was still flowing, but the energy was gone, replaced by the drunkenness of the crowd falling asleep on the couch or making out in the corner. This was the last place I wanted to be.

"Oh relax, I was just talking to Heather about my science homework, nothing else," Trevor said, defensively.

"She's not even in your class!" I shot back. I was angry but also incoherent since I'd been drinking for a while. "Can we just get the hell out of here?"

"Oh my God, can you just calm down?" Trevor said, his own voice rising, equally intoxicated.

"I'm sick of this! Let's go."

"No."

"Fine," I hissed. "I'll walk back alone." And then, Trevor turned away from me.

I left the party and began the long walk toward our dorm on the other side of campus. It was winter…in Syracuse. In my fury, I left without my coat, and I was wearing nothing but a skirt, tank top, and wedges. Shortly after I started my frustrated march, I stopped in my tracks, turned back in Trevor's direction, and upon seeing no one, I began to cry. I knew our relationship was headed in the wrong direction and the emptiness inside of me grew like a black hole.

The next morning, as I lay in bed recovering from the night before, my mind began to race. My thoughts were scattered and relentless, but when I got like this—hundreds of words forming all at once—I managed to find some sort of a solution for the problem I was facing. This time, I decided the only way I could regain any sense of control in our relationship was for me to stop drinking altogether and focus on my schoolwork.

I did exactly that, but in doing so, I withdrew even further from my friendships. During the first semester of my sophomore year, I was living in off-campus housing with a girl I met in writing class freshman year. We weren't close but she was nice and didn't seem to mind I spent most of my time at the apartment. I obtained a perfect 4.0 grade point average, making every excuse to sit in my room and read a book or study for an exam. Thing is, I was constantly alone and unhappy. I avoided any interaction with Trevor when he drank. Trevor had become a part of me over the past four years, and because of that, I felt like I was losing my identity as I withdrew into my own shadow. But I didn't have the strength to let go, and held on to whatever I could, whatever semblance of a relationship we had.

Then, during our spring break of that year when we were both home, Trevor asked if we could talk. I met him in the parking lot of the abandoned garage, and we both sat in my car.

"Hey, what did you want to talk about?" I asked. I knew the breakup was imminent, but I didn't think Trevor, after years of dating, would end it.

"I don't know how to say this," he started, his voice shaking. I could tell he didn't want to say what he was about to. "I'm just…not happy anymore. My spark is gone, and I know you're not happy either, Michelle. We need to break up."

Even though I was expecting this, I was devastated to hear him speak the words. "What are you talking about? We love each other, Trev," I pleaded. "It's been just us for years."

"I know, and I hate this."

"I just don't want to drink as much as you do. Are you going to throw this all away over that?"

"I've really tried. I can't anymore. I love you too but, I just can't." Trevor didn't sound fully convinced that the relationship was over, but he knew neither of us were happy.

"You're really going to end things like this?" I asked as I began to cry. "Don't do this."

"It's going to be okay, I promise. This is what's best for us."

"So, this is it?" I asked, defeated.

"I'm sorry. I'll see you around." Tears streamed down his face, something I had never seen before. He got out of the car and gently closed the door. He hesitated for a moment, and then disappeared into his own car, driving away into the dark.

I didn't move for another fifteen minutes, and kept my head pressed against the steering wheel as I sobbed. I felt lost and once again, abandoned. Trevor was there to help me navigate the pressures of schoolwork, the loss of Max, and my never-ending family drama. He was a good listener, and when I needed him, he was there for me. And now, he was completely out of my life.

Overwhelmed with heartbreak, I struggled to endure the pain, longing for relief. That night, I fell right into my mother's arms. I had never been so vulnerable around her, so exposed, but in that moment—in that feeling—I didn't care. If my mother wanted to cry with me, I let her. If she wanted to scorn Trevor, I let her. She offered comfort in a way that only a mother could, and at twenty years old, it was the first time in my life I was okay with it. And as she was doing so, I quickly learned how much grief was a part of life, how much I had to fight so that the depression, the same pain my mother felt day in and day out, did not take me over the same way it had her.

Chapter 12
What I Reached For

August 2003

It was not only my breakup with Trevor that helped repair my once broken relationship with my mother—being out of the house also gave me the space to breathe, to appreciate her more fully.

Our once combative nature toward each other seemed to dissolve with distance; it was as if sharing the same space had fueled our conflict. I began to regret the way we used to fight and made a conscious effort to nurture a more harmonious relationship with her even if we didn't always see eye to eye. I listened more and wasn't as quick as I was to react to my mother's indiscretions. Living apart had unexpectedly brought us closer together. I found a source of comfort that I'd never known before.

Even with this newfound support from Mom, I still felt a longing to form a bond with someone, anyone, after Trevor had left. I felt alone—too alone—and it was disconcerting, downright frightening. I had friends, but what I craved was the deep connection I formed while in romantic relationships. Friendships felt superficial to me, and I never quite felt secure enough to open up unless it was to someone I trusted and who loved me in return.

It was my first day of finance class junior year and I was sitting in the last row of seats surrounded by forty students or so. The teacher stood in the front of the room discussing the syllabus for the rest of the year, as I wrote in my notebook, barely paying attention to what he was saying. The agenda was something I could figure out on my own.

From right next to me, I heard a low voice. "What are you working on?" he asked, whispering so the teacher couldn't hear him. I had seen this boy in a few of my classes but never caught his name.

"Lyrics to 'Be Our Guest'," I whispered back. "Except I changed them to be sexy." I smiled coyly.

Chris was attractive, though not conventionally so. He was tall with curly dark brown hair and a goofy grin across his face. Just from that smile, I could tell he had a good sense of humor.

"Um, what?" He was now amused.

"It's the first day of class. We don't do anything anyway," I said. "Wanna read it?"

"Absolutely, I do," Chris replied as the teacher looked on suspiciously, but continuing with his introductory lesson. I ripped out the notebook paper and handed it to him.

After he read the lyrics, he wrote "Can I have your number?" at the bottom of the page. And just like that, I found myself in another relationship.

My abstinence from alcohol was now a thing of the past, and Chris and I spent most of our days at the bar or at his apartment, using the bitter Syracuse winter as our excuse for drinking so much. We had fun together, but it wasn't long until Trevor began to pop up in the back of my mind. My relationship with Chris wasn't the same, it wasn't as deep, but we had fun, and I enjoyed his company.

A couple of months into our relationship, Chris approached me and said he wanted to discuss our future. *Our future?* I thought. *What does that even mean?*

"I want to study abroad in Madrid," he said.

Whew! After a quick sigh of relief, two thoughts ran through my head: one, he wanted to ask me to go with him, or two, he wanted to break up with me.

"Oh, um, when do you want to go?" I replied uncertainly.

"I think next semester would be perfect. Do you think you'd want to come?"

I was pleasantly surprised by the invite but hadn't given a semester abroad much thought before he posed the question. Plus, I had a debilitating fear of flying so an eight-hour flight overseas wasn't exactly something I looked forward to. "I'll consider it," I replied, knowing I had already made my decision. Being alone was something I feared more than flying.

~

The Syracuse University study abroad program for business majors included a two-week bus trip from Amsterdam to our destination in Madrid, Spain. The trip itself was educational, and we visited multi-national companies along the way to learn about their business operations. About halfway through our trip, Chris and I, along with fifty other students, had just arrived in Switzerland. We had been traveling for about a week, and I was getting a bit homesick, but finding a great deal of enjoyment as I immersed myself in European culture. By this point in the trip, we had visited Amsterdam, Heidelberg, and Paris, and I discovered I had a sincere appreciation for the historical architecture and overall heritage of northern Europe.

It was a calm night in Geneva, and the setting sun illuminated the bustling sidewalks in an orange glow. I was surrounded by quaint storefronts and the steady flow of people—tourists casually snapping pictures of the scenery and locals hurrying to wherever they needed to be. Carla, a friend I had made during the trip, and I had just finished dinner at a local Swiss eatery and were walking back to the hotel where we were staying.

"They don't really serve much in terms of food here, do they?" I asked. "The cheese fondue tasted great, but man, I could go for a burger."

"Yeah, let's grab something at the hotel. We have to study for that exam tomorrow anyway," Carla reminded me.

"True. I'm hoping this is the first and last test of this bus trip," I responded as we continued down the street.

As we walked, we were still surrounded by tourists, but the crowd thinned as we approached the hotel. Then, as if a breeze of caution blew past me, I suddenly felt unsafe, though I couldn't explain why. I glanced apprehensively around us and then stopped in my tracks. Carla, who had taken another step or two before she realized I had paused, turned around to look at me.

"Do you feel like you're being watched?" I asked as the hair on the back of my neck stood up.

"Michelle, it's Geneva. I think our professor told us this is the safest city in the world," Carla reassured me and started on her way again.

"Yeah, well I hope so because I have a strange feeling," I said.

"Maybe it's the food we ate," Carla joked. I chuckled, though still felt uneasy.

Back at the hotel, Carla and I met up with her boyfriend, Alex, and Chris in their room. Books and notes were spread across the two double beds and the four of us spent the next few hours studying for our exam the next morning. As it approached midnight, I started to get sleepy.

"I'm exhausted," I said. "I'm going to head back to the room and go to bed. Do you want to come?" I directed my question to Carla.

"No, I probably should study a bit more," she said. "I'll read through this chapter and then head back."

"Okay, I'll see you all tomorrow," I answered. Then I gave Chris a quick kiss and left.

Carla and I shared a room on the first floor about three or four rooms down the hall from the front desk. When I got there, I changed out of my clothes but didn't lock the door as I knew Carla would be back soon. I sunk into the covers and fell asleep within minutes.

The next thing I knew, I heard a voice in the darkness, a voice that I did not recognize. The man didn't speak English but said something that sounded French. I slowly started to stir, still in that strange place between dreaming and waking.

Then, I heard another unfamiliar voice from across the room.

The first man spoke again, and I felt the bed sink in as he sat down next to me. He lifted the blanket and placed his hand on my upper thigh, stroking it gently as his plump lips grazed my cheek.

I finally came to, and the sudden realization that I wasn't dreaming made me jolt upright, my heart racing. I looked into the dark emptiness in front of me, but quickly, before I could make sense of anything, I collapsed back into my pillow.

When morning came and I opened my eyes, I felt something was off, not immediately remembering what had happened in the middle of the night. I noticed Carla moving around under the blanket in the bed next to mine and called out to her.

"Hey, Carla. I don't mean to wake you, but I'm not feeling great," I said grimacing. "And I have an awful headache."

"So do I. It's bad."

We both forced ourselves out of bed. *How am I going to take my exam feeling like this?* I thought as I massaged my temples in front of the floor length mirror next to the dresser. I did not consider this to be something way, way worse.

Carla turned on the shower. "My eyes are bloodshot," I called to her over the sound of running water. "This is strange."

"So are mine," Carla yelled back from the bathroom.

I poured my makeup bag onto the ground and opened my suitcase to grab a few clothes for the day. That's when I noticed many of my belongings were missing. "Hey, where's my camera?" I asked, becoming increasingly concerned.

"What do you mean?" Carla asked as she came out of the bathroom. She hadn't even gotten into the shower yet.

"I can't find my camera. It was right here last night," I said. "Do you know…"

"Oh my God, my wallet is missing," Carla said, cutting me off. It then hit her. "Michelle, we've been robbed."

I stared at her, the look of disbelief plastered on my face. "We need to get to the police right away," I said, slowly starting to recall what had happened hours earlier in the middle of the night. "I think we've been drugged."

And just like that, I felt like I was thrown into yet another high-pressure situation. I didn't stop to think; I rushed straight to the program director and explained what happened. Carla and I were taken to the local Swiss police right away.

The first police officer spoke English, but with a heavy accent. "What happened exactly?" he asked with a notebook and pen in hand.

"Well, I'm not sure, but we've been robbed. We both came back to the room after studying for the night and the next morning, our stuff was gone," Carla explained. "Why did they take only some of our things and not the entire suitcase?"

"These people are professionals," the police officer explained as he jotted down notes. "They get in, take what they want, and they get out of there."

"Well, not exactly," I cut in apprehensively.

"What do you mean?" he asked.

"I felt someone on top of me last night. I remember waking up but..." I stopped.

"But what, ma'am?" the police officer asked.

"I fell right back into my pillow," I said. "Like I was drugged with something."

"Ah I see," he said. "You two are Americans, no?"

"Yes, but what does..." I started to say.

"We will file a police report, but this happens more often than you would think, especially with tourists. There are no cameras on the building, and we were told the front desk did not see anything, so unfortunately, it would be impossible to find the perpetrators. Next time, I would suggest locking the door behind you," the officer said, taking a shot at Carla. It seemed as though they were sure we would never be back.

I couldn't believe what I was hearing. *How could anyone, let alone the police, seem to brush aside what I felt was a very serious offense?* Fear gripped me in this unfamiliar country.

Chris was there with me sure, but it quickly started to sink in that he was someone I had only met a few months prior. He was sympathetic though and he and his parents lent me quite a bit of money to help me get through the rest of the bus trip. All my credit and debit cards were stolen, and in 2004, there was no way to replace them quickly while overseas.

"Thank you for the money," I said as we lay in bed together one night. "I really didn't want to ask you, but I don't know who else to turn to."

"It's okay. I know you'll pay me back," Chris said.

"Yes, I promise to. My dad can give me money, but he has to use a payment services company, and I won't be able to get it until we arrive in Madrid," I said, feeling relieved but also that I was a burden.

"It's fine," Chris said.

"Thank you," I said again. Then, the details from the night before drifted into my thoughts. "Hey, do you think Carla and I were drugged?"

"I really don't think so. I'm sure the robbers came in, took what they wanted, and left. I don't think you should be worrying about this."

"Maybe," I said, though I was still uncertain. Everyone had been telling me to stop worrying, but deep down I knew I had to be given something to make me drop back into the pillow like that.

I started questioning everything. *How could something like this happen to me again? Did I just invite this kind of stuff into my life? Was there someone, something out to get me?* And the question that ran through my mind time and time again: *did he do more than kiss me?*

I didn't know what had happened after I lost consciousness, but I couldn't shake the memory of a man on top of me. The questions multiplied, but I, of course, forced myself to bury them. Eventually, I turned to my side and drifted off into a restless sleep.

Over the next few weeks, I applied for credit cards and worked with my father to open a new account. I eventually paid back everything I owed Chris and his parents, but money, as it usually does, caused tension.

"You said you'd pay me back last week," Chris said after class one day. "We've been in Madrid for two months and I have yet to see anything."

"I know, I'm so sorry," I apologized. "Something happened with the transfer from my dad, and it's taking longer than I thought. I've been on the phone with the bank for weeks trying to figure everything out. It's not easy!" I defended myself while at the same time realizing the irony of the situation. *Why couldn't I have empathized with my mother all those years ago?*

"Fine, do what you need to do. I'm going out tonight with the boys," Chris said tersely. "I'll talk to you tomorrow."

I had feelings for Chris but the strain on our relationship made me realize that I didn't love him the way I thought I could when we first started dating. I didn't care for him the way I did Trevor. When Chris told me he wanted to go out without me, I didn't feel uncomfortable; I felt relieved. I thought about ending the relationship the next night, but following the incident at the hotel, I felt too frightened to be so far from home without anyone to rely on.

In Madrid, I lived in a two-bedroom apartment provided by my host family in the Las Ventas area of the city. During the day, the neighborhood felt safe, crowded near the popular bull fighting arena, but at night, it was quiet, dark. Two nights a week, my last class ended at 9pm, so I bought some pepper spray and held it tightly in my right hand, my finger glued to the trigger as I made the ten-minute walk to the apartment from the Metro.

My host family was a generous couple, providing me with a full separate apartment two floors down from theirs. Dinner was on the table every night, and they did laundry for me once a week. They didn't speak English well (and I did not know much Spanish), so I relied on my roommate, Patty, to translate when we were together.

I enjoyed the time I spent abroad and even satisfied my internship requirement at a local Spanish company doing simple filing work. I traveled almost every weekend, be it with Chris or with friends, and the beauty of Europe's landscape and architecture captivated me. I immersed myself in the European way of life as much as I could, carrying that mace with me everywhere I went.

It was March 11, 2004, about halfway through the semester. I turned on the television in the kitchen of our apartment and sat down at the small round wooden table next to Patty. The news anchor spoke Spanish, but the program had English subtitles so I could read what was going on.

"With three days left until the elections, the bombing has left several dead. Details are still underway, but we have confirmed at least one hundred people have perished in this terrible tragedy."

The train bombings in Madrid rocked both the country and the world as it happened less than three years after 9/11. I sat there in shock watching the report and realized I myself had ridden that very same subway multiple times a day.

"This is horrific," I said to Patty.

"I know. We should stay home from class today," Patty insisted. "This could happen again."

"You're right," I replied. "I'm not getting on any public transportation today."

Thinking back, I don't remember if the school closed, or if I had just not gone to class, but I stayed at the apartment for a week following the attacks. I developed intense anxiety afterward, worrying that the worst could happen at any moment if I left the apartment. Everywhere I turned, I felt danger, sudden disaster lurking behind me.

Whatever anxiety I had following the bombings was short-lived though and I continued traveling to countries around Europe and spending my weekends partying at the discotecas until five in the morning. I found the food delicious, the people both beautiful and friendly, and the bull fights horrific. Despite the few setbacks, I had a wonderful experience overall.

After the spring semester in Madrid ended, I returned home to New Jersey, and Chris to his home in Rhode Island. We were still officially together, but I knew things weren't going to last. Dragging it out longer than I had to would not be fair to Chris, so I ended it a few days after we returned home.

The breakup wasn't difficult, at least for me—Chris took it harder than I thought he would—and though I was sad about the loss of yet another relationship, I didn't care about Chris the way I knew I should have. Plus, I had more important things to focus on when I returned home.

~

While I was away, Mom's financial situation had become untenable. She still worked at the catering hall, but was living paycheck to paycheck, and any unexpected expense brought her into even further debt. Her credit card limits had all been reached, and applying for further credit was impossible. She was essentially unable to spend any money unless she had cash, which was rare. The house was not being cared for, and she was unable to repair broken appliances. I found myself buying a countertop toaster oven because the main oven was unusable after it had stopped working. Sam had turned eighteen a few months prior, so child support was no longer a source of income either.

Mom had no choice but to file for bankruptcy. That and consequently being forced to sell the house were incredibly difficult for her. She held on to our home by a frayed string until one day, it was gone. The sale was hard for Dad as well, since the house was built by his grandfather and kept in the family for generations. Mom just couldn't keep up with the maintenance and other bills, and the selling of our home was just another nail in the coffin.

Though she spent years preparing for this day, Mom told me she never thought it would come to this. She pictured herself growing old in the house on top of the hill and possibly passing it on to us one day. Reality had something else in store though, and she now had to live out her days in an unfamiliar apartment on the other side of town. The process of moving out and downsizing so dramatically took an enormous toll on her well-being. The life she had created for herself was being torn away because of an illness she never wanted. I knew it wasn't her fault, but to her, it felt like everything was her fault.

The last night we spent in the house, Mom, Sam, and I sat on the empty living room floor, surrounded by boxes, our voices echoing against the bare walls. Teary-eyed, we reminisced about the good times we shared.

"The number of times we'd dress you up as a bride in that playroom," I said to Sam.

"Yes! Or when we'd dress Max up in those costumes. He hated us for that!" Sam said, laughing at the thought of our dog, a white curly-haired bichon frise, dressed up like a clown. I started to tear up thinking about him as the thought of my beloved Max brought a bittersweet wave of both happiness and sorrow.

"At least I won't have to deal with both of you destroying the basement to set up another haunted house," Mom laughed.

"Oh Mom, I'm really going to miss this house," I said. "We have so many memories."

"That's the whole point though, right? The memories?" Mom said, pausing to look at the fireplace. She always said it was her favorite feature of the house. "We'll be okay." Then she wrapped her arms around us as we sat there huddled together, each quietly sobbing so the others wouldn't hear our weeps.

But we all knew.

~

The next week, almost every piece of furniture from the house was auctioned. The apartment Mom relocated to was a quarter of the size of the house so it didn't have room for a ninety-inch dining table and eight chairs. Because both Sam and I were living on our college campuses by this point, Mom chose to rent a two-bedroom apartment so that we would have a place to sleep when we returned home for breaks or over the summer. When Sam and I were both home, Mom let us take the two bedrooms while she slept on the couch. While the apartment was small, it was comfortable and provided the basic necessities for a single woman.

To my surprise, the move didn't result in Mom entering another depressive state nor having to go to the hospital. She seemed to have prepared for this moment so that when it was finally over, she somehow welcomed it, even if it was still sad. There was no more worrying about the furnace breaking, or the refrigerator shutting down, or the roof leaking.

Rent prices were high, and without receiving any child support, Mom used her entire social security check to pay for rent and the mandatory living expenses. She didn't enjoy much in terms of financial freedom but at least she could more comfortably pay for groceries and gas, expenses that Aunt Gail had to cover for the past few months. If Mom had moved out of Nutley to a more affordable neighborhood, that may have caused more emotional damage than necessary, so she decided to remain in the town she knew, at least for the time being. While Mom received proceeds from the house sale, the majority were used to pay for some new furniture, and the remainder was given to my uncle for safekeeping. I never found out what happened to that money.

It didn't take long to unpack the moving boxes and settle into Mom's new living space that summer. Being in Nutley felt familiar and I was happy Mom decided to stay in town even if it meant she would be scrapping a bit more. It wasn't long before I started to reconnect with old classmates from high school and I found myself settling into a group of friends who I could enjoy my time with. Every weekend, we would get together and play beer pong in someone's backyard or visit a bar in town and dance all night to punk rock bands. It was a college summer I will never forget.

Then, there was Jack. Over the years, I could have been asked a hundred times why I was so attracted to Jack, but not once could I provide a concrete explanation. He was funny, wickedly funny, yes, but so were many of the other men I dated. He was good looking, with green eyes and dark brown hair, but again, so were a lot of my other boyfriends. I don't know what it was, but there was something about him, something indescribable, and I was drawn to him like a magnet.

Jack was part of my friend group, though not central to it, and would only come around every so often. I wasn't nearly as shy as I was in high school, but still too timid to do or say anything, let alone make a move, unless I had been drinking. And even then, I was still awkward.

It was a Friday night in July, and noticeably dark outside, the light of the moon obscured by the clouds floating in the sky. I walked out the back door of the house party and sat next to Jack on the steps leading to the yard. The rhythmic sound of the bass from the music could be heard coming from inside and it wasn't letting up.

"You good?" I asked. I had been drinking for an hour or so, and noticed Jack was quieter than usual, keeping to himself most of the night. When I noticed he went out to the yard by himself, I decided to follow him, and take my chance.

"Yeah," Jack replied only half listening. He was distracted by something and looked off into the trees that lined the edge of the property.

Then, some sort of invisible curtain lifted and he turned to me. "Hey, you wanna get out of here?" he asked. Normally, he was inattentive, but at this moment, his eyes looked directly into mine and there was this force that pulled me, unseen yet undeniable.

Back in high school we had class together, but I was dating Trevor at the time, so I didn't consider him more than a friend. Now, the way he looked at me on this hot summer night, I questioned everything. *Why had I never seen this side to him before?*

"Yes," I said.

The streets of Nutley were quiet, empty, peaceful. As we strolled side by side, his shoulders brushing up against mine at the most perfect moments, we didn't talk much, but it wasn't unpleasant. And when Jack grabbed my hand, folding his fingers into mine, I didn't pull away.

When we reached his father's house, he took two beers from the fridge, and we sat at the round glass table outside on the back patio. Before I could say a word, he looked at me, grabbed my shirt, and pulled me close to his lips.

"What are we…" I started to say.

Then, he kissed me.

It wasn't a simple kiss; it made my heart flutter in ways I never thought possible, something so unexpected—even Trevor didn't compare.

From that point on, I felt a deep personal connection with Jack. I don't know what it was about that night, but something came over me, and I couldn't ignore it.

Our fling only lasted a couple of months though. I tried—oh, how I tried—to turn whatever we had that summer into something more, but it never did and came to an abrupt halt when we left Nutley for our senior years on campus.

The first half of that semester was relatively uneventful. My mind was still focused on Jack, and I didn't feel compelled to start dating seriously. I went on a few dates, but none led to anything more than just that.

Christmas break came and went, and to my disappointment, there was no contact from Jack. I looked forward to reconnecting over the holidays while we were in Nutley, but nothing happened. I don't recall if I reached out to him and he didn't respond, or if I held back, expecting rejection. Either way, we didn't speak, and I realized I couldn't hold on much longer to something so uncertain.

I don't know what exactly drove my craving for stability and dependency in relationships. Maybe it was due to having an emotionally inconsistent mother, growing up in a chaotic household where I was endlessly expected to monitor her moods and adapt, never receiving that sort of predictability as a child. Or maybe I desperately sought to repair the damage I endured from the sexual assault so many years ago. Or maybe it was due to the divorce, knowing that love can vanish suddenly and I had to take care of myself emotionally. Back then, I had no idea, but as I reflect on that time now, I realize it was absolutely a combination of all three.

Chapter 13
Forward Motion

February 2005

I had just returned to campus after the holidays. It was a relatively calm wintry afternoon and the steady flow of flurries falling caught my attention as I sat on a bench inside the Hall of Languages. I admired the grand architecture of the buildings around me, and I was reminded of a snow globe I had flipped over and shaken so many times as a child. I was reading a book when another student walked up to me. He was attractive, with deep brown eyes and blond hair.

"Hey, are you ready for the...?" He stopped when I looked up and he saw my face.

"Am I ready for the, what?" I asked, confused.

"Oh, I'm sorry! I thought you were another girl from my class. Nevermind." He paused, continuing to look down at me as I started to blush. "I'm Kevin." He reached his hand out and I shook it. It was softer than I had expected.

"I'm Michelle."

"What are you reading?"

"Just some suspense novel," I said as someone opened the door nearby and a strong breeze whipped in. I wrapped my sweater close to my body. "Ooh, I can't believe how cold it's getting already."

"I heard there's a blizzard coming," he said.

"I hope not. I'm going to Chucks tomorrow for the games," I said, referring to my favorite bar on campus.

"You know what?" Kevin had a sly look on his face. "So am I."

"Oh yeah?"

"Yeah, I'll see you there." And then Kevin walked away.

I went back to reading my book, this time with a smile on my face. *Maybe it was time to move on from Jack.*

~

Chucks was near Marshall Street, the single strip of bars, restaurants, and stores situated two blocks from campus. The snowstorm did nothing to deter anyone from heading out, and the spacious bar was packed with hundreds of college students. Alternative rock played on the speakers overhead, and solo cups spilling over with beer lined the pong tables.

"These are for you," Kevin said as he walked up to me at the pool table in the back of the bar.

"Flowers?" I asked with a grin. "What am I going to do with these at Chucks?"

"Wait here." He walked over to the bartender. He came back with a pitcher, normally filled with beer, but this time, water.

"Here."

"Here what?" I asked.

"Put the flowers in this."

"Next time just get me the beer."

Kevin laughed. "Wanna play pool?"

"Sure."

My relationship with Kevin was textbook. We fell for each other quickly and easily. He gave me the attention, and more importantly, the security I needed. No games were played, like those that were played with Jack. I never questioned how much he liked me, like how I did with Jack. I never felt like I would be rejected if I asked him to hang out, like I did with Jack. But, oh, how I missed Jack.

But a relationship with Jack seemed impossible and I knew it was time to make room in my heart for someone else. Kevin and I spent every weekend together, be it out at the bars or hanging in at his apartment off campus. He wanted to spend as much of his free time with me as possible, and to me, that meant security. Kevin, like me, was also in his last year, finishing his degree in education. His parents lived just outside Binghampton in an area surrounded by farmland, something I found new and appealing coming from my home in a congested area of New Jersey.

It was nearing graduation, and we had been dating for about three months at this point. Kevin asked me out to dinner, and as we sat across from each other at the upscale Italian restaurant in downtown Syracuse, I felt awkward wearing the spring dress and the only pair of heels I owned. "So, I know you're looking for jobs in New York City after you graduate," Kevin said, lifting his glass of red wine, his lips stained.

"Yeah, that's where all the finance jobs are," I said, taking a bite of my chicken.

"You do know there are a lot of banks in Binghampton, right?"

I squinted. "What are you suggesting?"

"I spoke to my parents and well, would you like to move in with us after we graduate?"

The question had come out of nowhere. Kevin and I talked about continuing our relationship after graduation, but I never considered moving to upstate New York, especially since we had only been dating a short amount of time.

"Oh wow, that's uh, something I didn't consider," I said.

Deep down, I was hesitant but also happy that Kevin made things so easy for me. He reminded me a bit of Trevor in that way, and it had been years since I had that sort of stability.

"It's not like we have to get married tomorrow," Kevin said. He paused before continuing. "But that's not to say I don't want to one day." Then, he smiled at me.

I sat there for a moment, thinking to myself before responding. *What was there for me at home?* I thought about my parents, but for some reason, they weren't a driving force in my decision to move back. In fact, I felt somewhat compelled to stay far away. My father was busy with his two daughters, who were now seven and four, and my mother, who I kept in touch with every day, seemed to be doing well with the friends she made at work. Jack popped into my head, but he was very clearly out of the picture. My heart wanted to hold on, but my head told me to move on—I couldn't sit around waiting for him to reach out to me.

Sam was the only reason I'd want to move back to New Jersey, but she was busy in school. Plus, she and I spoke every day, and I knew Kevin and I wouldn't be living in upstate New York forever.

"Yes, I think I could make that work!" I said finally.

"I was hoping you'd say that!" Kevin's face lit up. "Should we order another bottle of wine?"

"Definitely!"

And we drank.

The next morning, the first person I called was Sam, who was now a freshman in college. Monmouth University was much closer to home but still, she decided to live on campus. Her reaction went as expected.

"Oh Michelle, how exciting! We all love Kevin!" she exclaimed. She had met him a couple times before and they got along.

Next, I called Mom. "Hey, I have news!" I said, still brimming with excitement after my call with Sam.

"Oh yeah? Tell me!" she said.

I was excited. "Kevin asked me to move in with him after we graduate. I think he's going to propose soon!"

"Oh, okay. That's fast Michelle, don't you think?" Mom asked, bringing my excitement to a halt.

"I know we've only been dating a few months, but he treats me so well, Mom," I said. "He's a good guy."

"Will you move to New York City?"

"No, I'll be living with his parents outside Binghampton. That way we can save up enough money to get married and buy a house."

"So, you're not coming back to Nutley?" Mom sounded upset, almost mad. I guess I was half expecting this, but after she had been in such a good mood this past year, I thought she would be happy for me.

"Not right now," I said. "His parents said they would give me a car so I can come visit all the time though."

"Oh, I see," Mom said, still disappointed. "Listen, I know you're in love, and I love Kevin too, but I think it's best if you come home. You're only twenty-two. This is ridiculous." Mom said it in a way that now made me angry, made me feel like I was being told what to do.

After several years of being forced to figure out everything on my own, I wouldn't acknowledge her reaction. I pushed back just like I had when I was a teenager and argued with my mother. I argued not because I thought it was the right thing for me to move to Binghampton, but because I was being told no, and that, to me, was unreasonable.

After I hung up, I called Dad, who I expected more pushback from. What's strange is that he encouraged it, saying something along the lines of "Michelle, that's fine with me." I'm not exactly sure why I expected a fight—maybe I wanted one to some extent—but I hung up without questioning it.

From that point on, I interviewed for jobs in and around the Binghampton area and accepted one working in the city center for a large bank. I wasn't making the money I would have in New York City, but it was more than enough for my needs at the time.

After graduation, Kevin and I moved into the basement apartment in his parents' house. His parents fell for me almost as much as he did and were happy to take me in. The apartment was fully furnished with a small bedroom and bathroom, kitchen area, and living space. It had its own entrance from the backyard and offered what I thought was enough privacy for the two of us to begin our lives together.

What I didn't expect were the visits from Kevin's mom at the end of each day. She often joined us down in the basement to watch a movie or cook dinner, sometimes startling me as soon as I walked in the door. I knew I would visit my own mother often, but this encouraged me to make the three-hour drive back to Nutley almost every other weekend. To me, Kevin's mother felt overbearing, and I didn't enjoy the company—I wanted my own space and getting away on the weekends to visit home was my way of doing that.

I did, however, appreciate that Kevin's parents never asked for rent, or any other expenses for that matter. They were very generous, offering me a reliable car, food, and a place to live for free. But with that, I essentially felt stuck. And although Kevin and I were making enough to pay for dinners and nights out, we put the remainder into savings for an eventual wedding. There was no way we could move out and find a place of our own.

Exactly one year after we started dating, Kevin made plans for a night out in New York City. It was a cold and snowy night, and I had to walk four long blocks in heels, barely saving myself from slipping on the ice that covered the sidewalks. We sat huddled in a corner of our favorite Spanish restaurant. It was dark, the candlelight casting a weak glow onto our faces, and I knew what was coming next. Kevin waited anxiously as the waiter came out with our champagne. There, sunk to the bottom of the glass, was the ring.

I looked at it, strangely disappointed that Kevin didn't get down on one knee as I had always pictured it as a young girl.

"Yes," I said and gave him a kiss.

The only way to get the ring out of the drink was to, well, drink it. Kevin picked up the glass by the stem, smiled at it, and chugged the champagne. After retrieving the ring, he placed it on my finger. I was twenty-three years old and engaged to be married.

I felt an odd mix of happiness and fear from that day on. To counteract the trepidation, I spent the next year and a half preparing for the wedding—searching for venues, picking out a cake, and choosing flowers. Most of the shopping I would have done with my mother, Sam, or my cousins who I chose as bridesmaids, I did alone. The day I found my wedding dress, I smiled faintly at the dress store owner while I stood on the podium alone, and she looked at me with sorrowful eyes.

About a month before the wedding day, I was alone in our basement living room. Kevin was out running errands, and his parents were on vacation on an island somewhere. I put my phone down on the coffee table, staring at it intently because I had one final decision to make before I could get married.

"Hey!" I said when Jack answered.

"Hey," he said, sounding a little surprised that I was calling.

"Yeah, hey sorry for reaching out like this. I don't really know why I'm calling." I felt embarrassed. "I just wanted to let you know that I'm getting married in a month!" I tried to sound excited, but it just came out incredibly awkward. I don't know what prompted me to pick up my phone that night. At twenty-four, I still had a lot to learn about expressing my feelings.

"Oh, wow! That's great!" he said, also sounding uncomfortable. "Anyway, how are you?"

"Good. Great!" I said, trying to make it sound like I didn't want him to fight for me.

"Okay, well, I'm happy for you, Michelle," he said, and we ended the conversation. I put the phone back down on the coffee table and felt like I was going to cry. *I'm so stupid!* I thought.

~

It was October 2007. The bridal party arrived the night before the ceremony for the rehearsal dinner and to practice walking down the aisle. It was warm and muggy, but the breeze from the lake kept our guests cool. The Old Kerry Manor rose high above the crowd, kissed by rays from the sunset as our wedding party prepared for the rehearsal. Groomsmen stood next to Kevin, the bridesmaids lined up at the back of the aisle with Sam as maid of honor and my half-sisters dressed in white as young flower girls. I was standing at the back of the line with my father.

The wedding coordinator lifted her hand as a cue for the first bridesmaid to begin. After she started, the coordinator shouted at her to stop and walk more slowly.

"Hey, Dad," I said looking up, just as I had done when I was a child, this time in heels.

"Hey, sweetheart," Dad said. And it was just the two of us for the first time since I was a child.

The wedding coordinator lifted her arm, signaling me to take my first step, but instead, a feeling of dread took over. I suddenly froze as the reality of the moment hit me. I clammed up, my heart started racing, and I grasped my father's hand tightly. The confusion on the faces of the bridal party glared at me, but I didn't say a word. What I wanted to do was scream, burst at the sudden feeling of panic I was experiencing, but instead, I thought about my family who had driven for hours to attend the wedding, about the disappointment my parents would feel, and about the money many of us had spent to make this day happen. There was no way I could walk away from this, no way I could make the decision that was best for me. I straightened up and a moment later, I took the next step, as the coordinator told me to speed up.

The next morning, I shook off the anxiety from the night before. The ceremony itself was picturesque, taking place in front of lake, which glistened in the sun. It was a brutally hot and sunny day for the time of year, breaking almost ninety degrees, and sweat beads dripped down my chest.

I lined up as I had the previous night with my father and since I felt the rush of anxiety then, the true walk down the aisle felt redundant. The lawn chairs in front of me were now filled with guests, and I focused on them as I made my way down. Dad kissed me on the cheek and handed me off to Kevin.

Neither Kevin nor I prepared our own vows and to my relief, the ceremony lasted no more than ten minutes. After the minister announced us as husband and wife, we kissed and joined the guests at the cocktail hour. I took pain relievers to help with the migraine that was forming.

Our honeymoon was adventurous, as we decided to take a month-long road trip around the United States. Not only did we want to see the country, but we wanted to find our next home, which Kevin decided would not be in New Jersey and I decided would not be in New York. In fact, I wanted to move as far away from Binghampton, and Kevin's mother, as possible. On our drive through South Carolina, I fell in love with Charleston, mesmerized by the beautiful beaches and the southern charm of downtown.

It was now January 2008, a month after our honeymoon road-trip ended, and we were both twenty-five years old. We quit our jobs and moved to a one-bedroom apartment outside Charleston. There was enough money saved to pay for expenses during the first few months, but we both found jobs quickly enough that we didn't need to use much of it.

The first year was exciting—being in a new place, meeting new people—and I discovered how much I enjoyed the south. The apprehension I felt during the ceremony subsided as the months passed. Kevin began working at a local school, while I was hired on the spot at a local law firm that made its money in asbestos litigation. They had a securities fraud division where I fit in nicely with my degree in finance. I worked long hours and spent my nights studying for the CFA exam, which would take years to complete. A few months after the move, we saved up enough for a down payment on a house in one of the suburbs outside Charleston called Mount Pleasant.

The house was a nice size and updated for 2008, with three bedrooms and two full baths. The front door led to an open living space and dining area near the back of the house. The kitchen was closed off from the rest of the house, but after living there for a few months, we spent most of our savings renovating and tore down the wall that separated it from the dining room. Upstairs, on either side of a large loft overlooking the living room, were two bedrooms and a small bathroom. The backyard was the perfect size for the four dogs—two mastiffs and two Yorkshire terriers—we had adopted over the years.

With house renovations, my job, and studying for the exam, I kept myself busy, rarely relaxing. Kevin was always on the go too, wanting to paint a bedroom, or look for a new car, or adopt a new animal. As much as I didn't think another pet was a good idea, I couldn't let the one-month-old kitten we found on the street outside our house go. Sadly, three months later, he died tragically when he got hit by a car and I cried for weeks.

I visited Nutley often. I don't know if it was because I missed my family or because I just needed to get out of the house with everything going on, but I would pack my suitcase every couple of months and head up north. My fear of flying worsened, so I would make the twelve-and-a-half-hour drive each way, even if it meant I had to go alone.

Our families visited us too. My mother, with little money and no one to accompany her, made the trip to Charleston once or twice a year, while my father visited once on his way to Disney with the kids. Sam started dating one of Kevin's friends, Zach, who lived closer to her in New York City, but because of this, they came to visit often. Unfortunately, Kevin's parents came to visit quite a bit too, and would stay for weeks on end, but at least it wasn't every day like when we had been living with them.

Sam and I remained close, but I hated being so far away from her. I couldn't simply grab a drink or head out for the night without making plans weeks in advance. I made a few friends while living and working in the south, but they felt more like acquaintances, a way to fill my time. The distance started to get too much for me, and in January 2010, two years after we moved, I started thinking more seriously about moving back north.

Then, I received a phone call from my mother. She was frantic. Sam was back in the hospital with another blood clot, and this time, it was even more serious. Sam, on the phone with me, scared but stable and alone in her hospital room, told me the story.

She had been visiting Dad in Nutley for the weekend and had just returned from a football game with friends. Sam had been drinking quite a bit at the game, so she went straight to bed. Not long after she fell asleep, her body jerked awake.

Sam walked downstairs and almost startled my father from behind. "Dad, I need to go to the hospital," Sam said, desperately trying to gasp for air. "I can't breathe."

Dad, who thought she was having an anxiety attack, insisted that she relax and take a deep breath.

"I CAN'T BREATHE!" Sam shouted. "We have to go!"

Jillian stayed back with the kids, while Dad and Sam got into the car, Sam wheezing the entire time. At the hospital, the doctors were able to stabilize Sam and performed a battery of tests and scans in the hours that followed. She was diagnosed with a pulmonary embolism and was told if she hadn't been drinking that night, because alcohol thins the blood, that the outcome could have been much worse. They treated her right away with a shot of blood thinners and Coumadin for six months. Sam was lucky to be alive.

I looked at my phone in disbelief. "Sam, I'm coming home," I said.

Chapter 14

The Way Back Wasn't Home

January 2010

After returning to Mount Pleasant following my visit to Sam, I sat down with Kevin and told him I wanted to move back to New Jersey permanently.

"But our jobs are here," he said, placing his glass of wine down on the table.

"We've quit our jobs before and have been fine," I said.

"That was before the recession."

"I know, but…" I started. "I miss Sam."

"I know you do, but she visits all the time," Kevin said. "We've made a life here and I love my job."

"I know and I love this area too. But we don't know anyone outside of work." I did love the southern charm, the beauty of the beaches in and around Charleston, but with no friends to enjoy it with, it started to become plain, boring.

"We aren't moving back," Kevin said. "We'll figure something out." He was not the pushy type, and we would often compromise, but when he wanted something, he'd most often get his way.

This fight wasn't the start of our troubles, but it was the start of my commitment to making a change.

Since we decided, or at least *he* decided, we weren't going to move back home, I spent the next few months making more friends at work and spending time out of the house, with or without Kevin. I started going to the gym and to parties that my coworkers hosted on the weekends—I was having fun. The apparent divide that began the night before our wedding continued to grow, and my feelings for Kevin started to dissolve.

On top of the disagreement about moving back home, it felt like Kevin started drinking even more than he had when we lived near Binghampton, causing a rift in our relationship. From my perspective, his drinking seemed to escalate, and it felt like he was now starting to drink most nights after work in a way that concerned me. At the same time, my need to settle down and start a family drove most of my decisions even if I didn't find myself perfectly happy. I made the most of whatever we had though as I tried my best to create a semblance of the marriage I had always envisioned. Unfortunately, Kevin's drinking was impeding on my sense of what that should look like.

"Hey, can we talk?" Kevin asked as he sat next to me on the couch in our living room holding an uncorked bottle of wine. He poured it into two glasses set on the coffee table.

"Sure, what's up?" I asked.

"We've been married for two and a half years now, and I think, well do you think, it's time to start having kids?" Kevin took a sip from his glass.

"Uh, I mean, are you ready?"

"Yes, absolutely!" he said, excitedly.

I paused. "Okay, if you want to start trying, then I think it's time you stop drinking so much."

"Oh, come on, I just drink to unwind after work," Kevin said. "It's nothing serious."

"Kev, you just said 'therious'," I said. "You don't need that much to unwind."

"I'm fine, Michelle. Relax and have a glass with me."

With that, I took the remote, changed the channel to my favorite show, and ignored his suggestion. Then I moved to the other end of the couch so as not to smell the rank odor coming from his breath.

It was at that moment I realized I could not continue this relationship, no less start a family with Kevin. I was neither shocked nor upset though; rather, coming to this realization brought me a sense of relief. It was almost as if I was hoping he would push back about his drinking, a way to give me a good reason to leave. The thing is, I was utterly terrified. I didn't have feelings for him anymore and I couldn't continue pretending, but this meant I would be alone, again.

The next night after work, I spent an hour cleaning the kitchen while our four dogs watched me curiously from the floor. When Kevin walked through the front door, it seemed as if he knew exactly what I was going to talk to him about. He sat down on the couch and turned the television off as I joined him.

"You already know what I'm going to say, don't you?" I asked.

Kevin nodded.

"I'm so sorry. I'm unhappy with my life and I can't do this anymore," I told him. "This person, who I've become, is not who I want to be."

Kevin's reaction was unexpected, but welcome. It came from a place of understanding as opposed to anger or sadness. "I know you're unhappy. I brought up children last night, and even though I didn't think you were in that space yet, I was hoping maybe you started to come around," Kevin responded gently. "But it's just not going to happen, is it?"

"No, and I'm sorry." I cried, but it was more because I was hurting Kevin's feelings as opposed to being inherently upset. I felt guilty for what could have been, but I also knew I could never go back.

"We'll figure it out. I'm sorry this is ending," Kevin said. "I'm sorry *we* are ending."

"Me too."

I knew I couldn't move forward with Kevin in my life, but I couldn't help but feel like my world was collapsing. I was only twenty-seven and already headed for divorce. Even though *I* knew it was the right choice, to everyone else, I would look like a failure.

The next few months were unusual to say the least. Since my name was still on the mortgage lien, I couldn't just quit my job without selling the house first. We depleted a lot of our savings during the house renovations, so I didn't feel comfortable with what we had saved to fully cover my expenses. Kevin and I worked it out that we live together until one, we sold the house, two, I could transfer to the New York City office at my current job, or three, I could find a new job back home.

During this time, I decided to stop studying for the CFA exam and focus on the move. I started hanging out with friends from work more often, and Kevin did the same. It was as if we were now roommates, living our own separate lives, and it all happened within a couple weeks.

Right before the holidays, about two months after Kevin and I agreed to separate, I was at my desk working on a claims document. I looked up at my computer after I heard a ping—Jack, the boy who never left my head, had signed onto instant messenger. I looked at the screen for a few minutes, playing out possible scenarios in my mind. *What do I do here?* I thought. I was told it could take months to finalize the divorce, but I was still married. *What would other people think? They'd look down on me for sure.*

But what did I think? In my heart, I felt that I was single, that Kevin and I no longer cared for each other in that way. *Isn't that all that mattered?* I wasn't hurting Kevin—he had moved on, and I got the sense he started talking to someone from work. *Plus, what was there to lose?* I had already lost everything anyway.

"Hey!" I wrote. "Long time."

"Wow, blast from the past. How are you?" Jack asked. We hadn't spoken since I called him a month before the wedding. "How's married life?"

"I'm pretty good," I said. "Married life, not so much." I was relieved that he brought up the topic I so badly wanted to discuss.

"Oh yeah?"

"Yeah, Kevin and I are getting a divorce."

"What happened?"

"We just weren't happy and I realized I may have rushed into the whole marriage thing." I felt ashamed.

"Are you still in South Carolina?"

"Yeah, I have to stay here until we sell the house."

"Listen, I'm sorry you are going through this, and I hate myself for saying this, but…" Jack stopped typing. After a few seconds, he resumed. "…but I'm happy to hear this."

"You are?" The wave of elation took over. In an instant, my feelings, the feelings that never truly left, were validated.

"When you left for college the summer before our senior year, I thought you'd be back," Jack said. "But then you got married and moved away."

"I know I did," I said. "I didn't think you even liked me anymore."

"You didn't think I liked you?! Michelle, I was falling for you."

"You never responded to my texts," I said. "I even invited you to visit me in Syracuse, but you never did." *Did I miss something?* I thought.

"It was stupid of me not to come," he responded. "But it would have still been long distance, so what was the point?"

"I guess, but I took it as you didn't want to see me."

"You and I…we were more than just a fling," Jack said. "You broke my heart when you ran off and got married."

"You know, I never stopped thinking about you," I typed with sweaty palms.

"You think I stopped thinking about you?" he wrote back. "I miss you…a lot."

My heart started to flutter. The connection I felt more than five years ago was still there and his words caused the spark to re-ignite.

"I called you! Before I got married—do you remember that?" I asked.

"Of course I do," he wrote. "But what was I supposed to say? Don't do it?"

"Yes!" I shouted at the computer as I wrote the words.

"Michelle, I couldn't do that."

"I know. It was just…that's all I wanted to hear. Instead, I made a huge mistake."

"Well, hopefully we can fix that."

The flirting continued for the next few weeks. Every day, I'd go to work and sign on to messenger hoping to see Jack's name, and every day, he'd be there. We'd reminisce for hours, talking about high school and summer breaks, or banter back and forth about our feelings for each other. Plus, the feelings Kevin and I had for each other were too far removed, and neither Kevin nor I seemed to mind.

"So, how's your new man?" Kevin questioned me when I walked into the kitchen after work one evening. Kevin and I had formed an unusual friendship after the decision to separate, and I told him about Jack. He seemed to take it in stride; not once did he argue with me, nor did he make me feel uncomfortable for ending our relationship. Not once did we speak of the night when I sat him down asking for a divorce. It was odd but also easy for me, so I refrained from questioning it, up until now.

"Are you okay with all this?" I asked, hoping I didn't unintentionally open a can of worms. "I don't want to make it weird or hurt your feelings in any way."

"Oh, believe me, the weirdness is too far gone to go back to what it was. It's fine," Kevin said. "Is your job letting you transfer?"

I was relieved. "My boss is still working on it, but it's looking good. As long as the transfer to the New York City office goes through, I should be out of here in a couple weeks."

"Okay, take your time," Kevin said. "There is one other thing though."

"Sure, what's up?"

Kevin became timid but went ahead. "I wasn't going to ask you for this, but I worked hard and spent a lot of money on the engagement ring I gave you." He paused to take a breath. "Do you think I could have it back?"

I didn't give it a second thought. "Of course you can." Since I had taken the ring off a couple weeks ago, I went upstairs to the guest room where I was now sleeping to retrieve it and handed it back to Kevin. "I'm sorry we didn't work out," I told him.

He smiled.

~

I spent the next week packing and finalizing plans to move home. My request for a transfer was approved, but my boss was not prepared to meet the cost-of-living increase, so I had to live with one of my parents until we sold the house or I found a higher-paying job. This wasn't ideal, but it was the only option, and I decided that living with my father was the better choice. It's not that I didn't enjoy seeing my father, Jillian, and the kids, who were now teenagers; it was that I had been living on my own for nine years now, and the thought of being under someone else's roof, with their rules, made me feel trapped.

I did consider living with my mother, but after I thought about how much better our relationship was when we lived separately, I decided it was best I keep it that way. Mom did express some disappointment, but told me she understood, and in the end, she was just happy I was moving closer to home. In fact, it seemed both she and my father supported my decision to leave Kevin.

Now that the move was confirmed, I wanted to share the news with Jack.

"Hey!" I pinged from my office in South Carolina.

"Hey, my girl, what's up?" Jack pinged back.

"I have some good news!" I was genuinely excited.

"Oh yeah? You get another dog?" Jack joked.

"Ha, nope. I'm moving back to Jersey."

"Like, Nutley?"

"Yep! I can transfer to the New York City office and will live with my dad and stepmom until we sell this house."

"Oh, okay, that's nice."

And just like that, my heart sank. *What the hell kind of response was that?* We had been talking for weeks, and he made it abundantly clear he wanted to see me. I took a minute, and a breath, and began to type, hoping I mistook his response.

"Yeah, it'll be great. Maybe we can make plans to hang out?" I suggested.

"Yeah, maybe," Jack wrote back, but then, signed off.

He had been so forthcoming with his feelings that his sudden lack of interest took me by surprise, and there it was—the insecurity that tipped off my racing anxiety; my safety net seemed to be ripping apart thread by thread. I felt like I was hurtling toward the edge of a cliff, yet I had few places left to turn.

I didn't change my mind about leaving though. A week later, I drove with Kevin and Gizmo back to Nutley after saying goodbye to my other three sweet dogs, crying intensely as I hugged them. The mastiffs were too large to take back with me, and our other Yorkshire terrier was closer with Kevin. When we arrived at my mother's, Kevin gave me a clumsy yet friendly hug before I rang the doorbell. He then continued on his way up to visit his family's house in Binghampton for the week, never looking back.

Coming home to Mom was nice. She expressed her happiness that I was back in town. However, and though I couldn't explain it, I felt a sense of pressure being so close again. Her emotional baggage was still apparent and having me home meant she had a place to store it. Regardless, she welcomed me with open arms as soon as I opened the door.

Later that day, I settled into Dad's house, taking the spare bedroom on the second floor. Dad's house was filled with boxes, kids' toys, trains, and antiques, and it felt claustrophobic. I tried to clean my room as best I could, but my father refused to let me throw anything out and I had nowhere to put the mounds of clutter that covered the floor. I unpacked my suitcase and placed the few items I took from South Carolina on the few empty shelf spaces I could find.

Then, I sat down on my twin bed and thought about the relationships I've had over the years, each one completely unique. Oliver, Trevor, Chris, and Kevin all taught me about love and commitment in their own different ways. Though, as I reminisced, I found there was one thing that remained constant across all of them—I blamed myself for each breakup. I blamed myself for each of the heartaches I caused. Even when I didn't initiate the breakup, I looked at myself, and only myself, as the reason for being alone. I resolved my next relationship would be different, and it would last. I promised myself that I would hold onto something in my life for good.

I texted Jack.

~

Jack and I sat beside each other on the parking lot curb outside his apartment building in Nutley. He looked exactly the same since I last saw him that summer six years ago. It was dark and cold, but I was wearing a coat and a blue wool hat to keep me warm.

"I'm happy you're back home," Jack said. "I'm just not the relationship type."

After everything I had been through, I wouldn't let him do this to me. I pushed back. "What are you talking about? What happened to everything you told me when I was living twelve hours from here?"

"Like what?" Jack asked as if our previous conversations never happened.

"Like how you missed me and how you wanted me to move back home to be with you. Was it all a lie?"

"Well, no. I did miss you. I'm just not ready for something like this," Jack explained. "I've never been in a relationship before, and I like my single life. I don't like having to answer to anyone."

"Okay, well what do you expect from me? To wait around until you're ready?" I asked. "I won't do that." I knew full well that I was bluffing.

"I understand."

"Okay then. I guess I'll see you around." We ended the conversation then and there.

I drove back to my father's house and called Sam. "Hey, are you around tomorrow?" I asked.

"Sorry, no I'm at Zach's in the city," Sam said. She was still dating Kevin's friend, and I don't know for sure, but I felt she blamed me for the divorce. She was never outright angry at me for leaving Kevin, but there was something there, a hint of disappointment woven into her silence.

I talked to Sam for a few minutes before hanging up. As I sat there alone on my bed, I could hear the laughter from my father and sisters in the living room downstairs. I was only a few steps from where they were, but I felt like I was still eight hundred miles away.

I spent the next two days searching for jobs and working with my attorney to sell the house. As I filled out applications, I felt empty inside. I had no one to turn to.

Then, I got the call from Jack.

"Hey," he said.

"Hi."

"I thought about what you said," he started to say. "And I can't not be with you. I want you in my life, Michelle."

And the anxiety floated away.

~

Two months later, in April of 2011, the house in South Carolina was sold for the same price Kevin and I purchased it for. Considering we bought it before the housing crash of 2008 really took hold, we were lucky we didn't lose money on it. After real estate fees and other expenses, I received proceeds of about fifteen hundred dollars, money I put directly into savings. Coinciding with the sale of the house, I found a risk analyst position at a large company in New York City and accepted it right away. This meant I could now afford to rent a place of my own, and I moved out of my father's house a month later.

The one-bedroom apartment I found in Nutley was close to both Mom at one end of town and Dad at the other. It was small and needed updating but the landlord accepted dogs, one of my requirements since I brought Gizmo home with me. The living room, just big enough to hold a small couch and television, flowed into the hallway to the moderately-sized bedroom and bathroom. Between the two rooms, there was a galley kitchen with outdated but functional appliances.

My relationship with Jack progressed well for the next few months and we grew close, but Jack's attitude was different, nonchalant, a stark contrast from my more recent relationships. The strange thing is, I was drawn to it, attracted to the detachment even if I found myself constantly anxious, not knowing if he was as committed as I was. One day, he would spill his heart out to me, and the next, it would be like I was holding him back. This never-ending battle between my passion and his indifference led to a gradual deep distrust and lack of security. But I held on because I was lost in him. He had this pull that wouldn't let go and when it did, I broke.

"Hey, do you want to hang out tonight?" I asked one Saturday afternoon about six months into our relationship.

"I'm golfing today," Jack answered.

"Again?"

"Yeah. I'll be back this afternoon. I'll probably want to chill when I get back but we can hang if you want."

"Okay. I'll text you later," I said, anxiously questioning his intentions, whether he wanted our relationship to work or not.

Later that afternoon, when Jack had said he would be back, I texted him, "Hey, what do you think? Wanna meet up?"

"Oh hey, my friends wanted to head for beers," he responded. "I'm already out."

"Oh, who?"

"Friends from work," he said. "We're at a bar in the city."

"Well, what do you think if I meet you there?" I felt like I was pulling at strings.

"No, it's the guys," Jack wrote back. "Just let me be."

"What do you mean, let you be? I haven't seen you in weeks."

"I'm just not around tonight. I'll talk to you tomorrow."

"Okay I'm sorry. It's fine."

Our relationship was a constant struggle, and any tension led me to repeatedly apologize, keeping the illusion that we were on good terms. I felt that I had to be perfect to be loved and my brain was hardwired that safety meant commitment and predictability. When the fear of abandonment crept in, it only made me even more committed.

And maybe, just maybe, I was meant for the chaos.

I didn't sleep that night and the fear of him cheating took over my thoughts. I had no proof though. When we were together or out with our mutual friends or spending the night alone in my apartment, we were strong, but as soon as I started to feel somewhat secure in our love for each other, Jack would pull away. The rope was tight though and as soon as he was more emotionally available, I wouldn't hesitate to jump back into his world. It was easy for Jack—he had nothing to fight for.

"Hey, you wanna go out to eat tonight?" Jack asked. "I think we should check out that new place on Chestnut." There was no mention of our conversation from three days ago.

"Yeah sure," I said. "Pick me up at seven?"

The two of us sat in the back of the restaurant, away from the busier bar area.

"How was your night out in the city?" I asked.

"It was fun," Jack said.

I wasn't going to bring up what I said next, but the stress I felt over the past few days wouldn't let me stay quiet. "I saw a picture of you with Maria," I said. "I thought you said it was just the guys."

"Yeah, some girls met up later in the night. It was no big deal," Jack answered sternly. "Why do you always accuse me of cheating?"

"I didn't accuse you of cheating. You told me something different the other day and I found out through a friend's post that you were with your ex. I'm upset."

"Listen, you just don't trust me and I'm sick of it," he said angrily.

"Okay, hey, I'm sorry I said anything. I trust you wouldn't do anything. I just wish you told me."

"No, I'm just done."

"What do you mean, you're done?"

"I think we should head home," Jack said.

I had no choice but to end our dinner and we walked out to his car without saying a word. Jack drove me back to my apartment, the car silent, but as soon as we reached my door, something changed in him.

"Can I come up?" Jack asked.

Did he just ask me that? I thought to myself. I turned to him, smiling as my heart could no longer be felt pounding against my chest.

"Of course."

Our relationship pendulum swung like this for another few months until the forces holding us together were no longer strong enough. Jack permanently ended our fourteen-month on and off affair the following spring.

It wasn't the marriage, the promise, the vows that broke me. It was this. Looking back, the red flags were everywhere, but I just couldn't see them, or more likely, I didn't want to see them. At the beginning, when I moved back from South Carolina, I promised myself that I wouldn't let this relationship die. But here I was, digging the hole and burying it like I did everything else in my life.

And I, of course, blamed myself.

C h a p t e r   1 5

Learning How to Stay

August 2012

For months after my breakup with Jack, I fell into depression, feeling like I somehow hit a new low, and it terrified me. The feeling was similar to when I broke up with Trevor, but this time I was older, almost thirty. Back when I was with Trevor, I told myself I'd be married with kids by now. But here I was, back in Nutley where it all started, single with no one I wanted to be with.

I felt like I was drifting into a black hole, and I didn't know how to escape the feeling. I lost my appetite and could only feel a debilitating sadness for months. Falling asleep was easy for me since I was so tired by bedtime, but I'd usually wake a few hours later and lay in bed with a racing heart, my body feeling like it could give up on me at any moment until I somehow drifted off to sleep again.

For the first few moments after I woke up, I would suddenly feel normal, painless, but then the wave of sorrow would hit like a truck. I tried in every possible way to get rid of the agony that controlled me. When it got bad, I would bring Gizmo and spend the night at Mom's apartment just as I had done when I broke up with Trevor, wanting her company and knowing she would understand.

When I did so, I couldn't help but question if this was how my mother felt for most of our lives. I wondered if she felt this constant deep pain in the pit of her stomach, if she wanted to rip her heart out of her chest because of how unbearable it was. The guilt of how I used to treat her steadily set in.

Unlike my mother though, my pain was relatively short-lived and when I was able to eventually move on, it seemed as if I was ready to face any strikes that flew at me. I had seen what my mother endured, the depression that controlled her life, and I refused to let the same happen to me, even if it felt impossible.

About five months went by and I started to feel myself again. Though waves of grief hit, they became fewer and farther between with each passing day. I found ways to find comfort through distractions at work and with friends, and by dating around to help keep my mind off the one I still wanted.

Sam had walked into my apartment without knocking and grabbed a bottle of water from my fridge. Then she plopped down onto the carpet and sat cross-legged near me on the couch. Gizmo ran up to her, wagged his short stubby tail, and jumped into her lap.

"How are you doing today?" Sam asked, sympathetic. By this time, Sam had broken up with Zach and had moved into New York City with two other girls she met online, turning a one-bedroom apartment into a three-bedroom with the help of a portable room divider.

"I'm still feeling a little down, but much better than I have been," I said, taking a sip of the tea I had prepared and bringing the woven blanket draped over my legs closer to my body.

"I'm really happy to hear that," Sam said, rubbing my dog's ears.

"Plus, I'm starting to date here and there. Nothing serious, but it's helping."

"Oh yeah? With that guy from work?"

"Yeah. Well, no, with this guy Paul, who's friends with Brandon from work," I said. "We are going out together this weekend."

"Oh, that's great!" Sam said. "I'm glad you're getting out there."

"Yeah, I'm having fun."

"Well good, because I wanted to talk to you about something." Sam handed Gizmo to me as she moved over to the couch where I was sitting.

"Sure, what's up."

"My lease is up at the end of the month, and I was wondering if you'd want to move to Hoboken with me. I need to get out of the city," Sam said. "I think I need to be with someone I can trust."

Sam and I remained close, almost too close after all the hardship we endured in our lives. Sam often kept her emotions to herself though, much like me, but this time, it seemed like she was finally opening up.

"What do you…is everything okay?" I asked.

"Yeah," Sam said. She stopped speaking, but I could tell something was up.

"Tell me, what is it?"

"I've been having panic attacks, Michelle. I wake up in the middle of the night and can't sleep. My heart starts pounding and it feels like I...I can't breathe," Sam confided.

"I mean after everything you've been through, that makes sense. What do you think causes them?" I wanted to ask a million more questions but held back.

"I just think about our lives and how they could have been so different."

"Okay, listen to me. What we've been through, it's a lot. The life we've experienced—it's not healthy for anyone. It's completely understandable and I'm here for you."

Sam smiled. That's all she needed to hear. "So, are you saying you'll move in with me?" Sam wiped away a tear from the corner of her eye.

"Of course," I responded. "And if you ever feel like that in the middle of the night, call me. I'm here. I've always been here."

Though I would never admit it, I was having panic attacks too. For one, I was still healing from the breakup with Jack, but in addition to that, I felt so incredibly lost. Without the safety of steady boyfriends in my life, and although I was physically surrounded by family and friends, I felt isolated.

~

Paul was outgoing and expertly flirtatious, so it was easy for me to succumb to his charm and wit. He had no qualms about telling me I let off a "good energy" while looking directly into my eyes.

A few hours before our date, I spent an hour at my apartment getting ready. I put on wedges and a green autumn dress that flowed when I spun. Even though I hated wearing heels, I felt as though this occasion warranted them. My makeup was elegant enough to include my rarely worn red lipstick, and I curled my hair so the blonde flowed in front of my hazel eyes. My final touch was the spritz of perfume I bought myself after tossing the bottle from Jack.

Alone in my apartment, I reached for a shot glass from the cabinet over the sink. I poured the tequila from the bottle sitting on the laminate countertop and gulped it down without second-guessing my decision. Quickly though, I grabbed a glass, filled it with water from the faucet and gagged before I chugged it. Tequila was something I would have to get used to.

I waited on the front steps of my Nutley apartment complex in the dark moonlight as the headlights from the gray Honda appeared. Dad opened the door from inside and greeted me with a kiss on the cheek.

"So, you're going to the city by yourself tonight?" he asked. I hadn't seen Dad in weeks, but mainly because I didn't want to see anyone.

"Yeah, I'm just meeting up with some friends. I should be back before midnight."

"Okay, have a good time."

Dad dropped me off at the station at the other end of town and waited until the train pulled away before heading home. Sitting alone in my seat with my makeup perfect and hair done up, I felt out of place. I clutched my purse tightly wishing I had brought the mace that I had been carrying with me for almost ten years now since my trip to Europe but learned that I could always stab someone with my keys if anyone came too close.

Hoboken was three stops away from Nutley, and there I could catch the PATH train into New York City. When I reached the PATH station, it was hot and muggy, and I began to feel my eyeliner run and the sweat beads form on my neck. I started to feel nervous, wondering if meeting up with Paul was the right decision.

I continued forward.

When I reached my destination, I exited the PATH station and hiked seven blocks to lower Manhattan. I turned the corner and trekked down the street where the bar was located, the one where I was meeting Paul. I found it difficult to walk in heels down the long cobblestone alley, which was bustling with patrons and smokers who were hanging outside the several bars that lined the street. I saw Paul standing in front of the restaurant with two of his friends.

"Hey, there she is!" Paul called out to me. His friends followed his gaze, making me feel embarrassed and I immediately felt like I was going to trip and fall in front of the crowd.

"Hey, sorry I'm late," I said, not sure if I should hug or kiss him on the cheek. I went for the hug. Paul, of course, went for the kiss.

"No problem at all. This is Justin and Wayne. The rest of us are upstairs," he said. "Let's go." He took my hand and led me to the elevator that took us to the rooftop bar of one of the most exclusive restaurants in New York City.

During our night together, Paul and I shared mindless stories about which bands we liked in high school or why armadillos were my least favorite animal. We were heavily flirting, and I was enjoying myself. About an hour into the date, I excused myself and took a few minutes in the bathroom.

"Why would someone like this want me?" I whispered to myself as I looked in the mirror.

"Oh, honey, you are gorgeous!" I didn't see the other woman emerge from the stall, and after a quick startle, I said, "Thank you," gave her a warm smile, and walked out of the bathroom with renewed confidence.

The alcohol flowed and I loosened up the more I drank. It was when Paul put his arm around me that I felt those butterflies again and realized I could feel the pang of happiness with someone else even if we had only been introduced a week earlier by a friend from work. I once again felt wanted, assuming one thing would lead to another and I'd end up in yet another long-term relationship, filling the void that made me feel so empty.

We kissed from the moment we walked through the front door of his penthouse suite, through the living room and onto his oversized bed. He picked me up in his arms almost too easily and I felt weightless, wrapping my legs around his waist. I was surprised by how strong he was but welcomed it. This was new to me, but I was drunk and I told myself I could handle it.

The next morning, I slipped out of bed, put on my green dress that was sprawled across the floor, and touched up my makeup in the large white marble bathroom, impressed by the clear glass that surrounded the shower and the clawfoot tub that stood next to the double sink. I made my way back to the bedroom, where I found Paul still in bed. I hadn't noticed the view of Central Park in the darkness of the night, but now that I saw it, I was astonished at how beautiful it was.

"Hey, you want to grab some breakfast?" I asked, fully expecting we would make a trip together to the diner down the street to grab a bagel or a cup of tea. Paul stirred from under the sheets and looked up at me. I was now sober and suddenly felt self-conscious.

"Oh, hey, I can't. I have plans today."

"Oh, okay. That's fine," I said as I suddenly no longer felt the confidence I exuded a few hours earlier. "I guess I'll head out now."

"Yeah, here, let me show you to the way out."

Paul crawled out of bed, threw on some slippers, and walked me through the living room to the front door. His personality had shifted dramatically from the sweet, enthusiastic man I was talking to the night before to this more passive, disinterested person I didn't recognize. I hadn't felt this kind of shame in a long time.

Then suddenly, out of nowhere, a flashback hit and I was sitting next to Ian on the sand dunes. The memory had remained dormant for years but for some reason, there he was, forcing my hand down his pants. I couldn't explain why I thought of him then, but I did. The secret I had kept for sixteen years made me feel so alone. Over the years, I tried to lock it as far away as I possibly could, but it was inevitable that Ian and David would sometimes claw their way back into my mind when I was least expecting it. At almost thirty years old, I suddenly realized how profoundly both of those boys, those simple teenage boys, affected every relationship I had ever been in.

The flashback was gone, and even though the moment was fleeting, I made a promise to myself that morning, a promise that I would never break. I vowed that anytime I thought of that memory, I would feel not shame, but strength. Whatever choices I made that night with Paul were my own, and I made a resolution that Ian and David were not going to dictate how I felt after making them. I looked at Paul, and turned around, walking away with my head held high. I never spoke to him again.

For more than fifteen years after I was assaulted, I searched for safety and validation, maintaining mostly long-term relationships. After this meaningless one-night stand with Paul though, I now felt that I needed to address this sense of shame that I had kept buried for so many years. I decided I was going to explore this newfound sexuality on my own terms, proving that I could decide what was right, and at the same time, what was wrong for myself.

~

Sam and I moved to Hoboken that fall of 2012. The apartment I shared with her was small, but that was nothing new to us. The front door opened to an eat-in kitchen large enough to fit a small round table and two chairs. The brown floor tile and chipped countertop matched the outdated appliances and drop ceiling, and the open space living room was just big enough to fit a loveseat and small credenza. Other than the bathroom where someone sitting on the toilet could touch both the sink and the shower at the same time, there were two enclosed bedrooms, neither with windows. It was clear the building hadn't been updated since it was built in the fifties and the cracks in the wall needed to be plastered, but neither of us minded.

The tie that bound Sam and I never really loosened, and we spent most of our nights and weekends together. Though we hadn't lived together for over ten years, it was like we never stopped.

"We're going to grow up and be like those two women. Oh, what were their names?" Sam asked excitedly.

"Thelma and Louise?" I said laughing.

"Yes! Thelma and Louise!"

"I do hope they aren't the ones who drove off the bridge," I joked.

"I think they were. Anyway, are you headed to The Factory tonight?"

"What do you think?"

The Factory was a popular bar in Hoboken, known for its up-beat music, friendly atmosphere, and constant flowing alcoholic beverages. The long, narrow front area, lined with the stocked bar on one side and mirrors on the other, led the way to the back area, which was more open with tables and people dancing. Along the upper half of the walls were a multitude of televisions, always tuned to some sports channel.

The bar became my sort of second home where I made friends, the ones who I could laugh and have a good time with, not the ones where I felt obliged to expose my past. With them, I felt unrestrained, cracking jokes that walked the thin line where I could possibly offend someone else with an off-the-cuff remark. But no one was ever offended.

It was a clear Sunday afternoon in February 2013. The basketball game was playing on the televisions overhead, and the bar was packed, filled with patrons shouting obscenities at the screens and high fiving their neighbors. Drinks were being spilled everywhere, and other bar-goers were shoving their way through the crowd. I *loved* it.

Sam was at the bar, but at the other end talking to one of the bartenders and her new boyfriend, William. I looked over at her and smiled, and then turned to my friend, Bella. "Do you want to do a shot with me?" I asked. She had long blond hair, deep green eyes, and I was attracted to her no-nonsense yet kind attitude.

"Absolutely!" Bella said.

"I got them," Andrew interrupted. "Three shots of tequila on my tab."

"Andrew! Where have you been?" I asked. "And thanks for the shots."

Andrew was a regular at The Factory and since I had become one myself, we hung out quite a bit. He was tall with brown eyes, messy hair, and a sly smile that made me wonder what he was hiding.

"I was seeing someone," Andrew said. "Didn't work out though." He was nonchalant about it, and the breakup didn't seem to bother him one bit.

The day I met Andrew, I found him instantly attractive and was happy to hear he was single again. "Oh, this makes me so happy," I said, quickly realizing I may have let on too much. "Not that you broke up with your girl, but that you're back."

Andrew chuckled. "Eh, I didn't really like her. You're much nicer," he said coyly.

"Okay you two, save it for the bedroom," Bella said, butting in.

"Oh, he wishes," I added sarcastically.

"I do," Andrew said more seriously. I looked at him with intrigue and the three of us clinked glasses and took the shot.

Laughs turned into dancing, dancing turned into kissing, and before I knew it, I was back at my apartment lying next to Andrew in a double bed, the biggest size I could fit into my bedroom. I was drunk, but happy and this time, ready to take control.

And then I did.

~

"Well how did that happen?" I said jokingly after our escapade was over. I threw on a pair of sweatpants to sleep in.

"Tequila shots, in the middle of the afternoon," Andrew quipped back.

"Probably," I said, chuckling. "Okay definitely. Maybe next time we take them after the sun goes down."

"Good idea."

We let the alcohol take us to sleep. The next morning, I got dressed for work as Andrew slept soundly since he didn't have work that day. Without waking him, I slid out of bed, brushed my teeth, chugged a full glass of water, and threw my messy hair into a bun. The hangover made my head throb and my eyes felt heavy, but going to work like this had become the norm, and I closed the door behind me with my laptop bag in hand.

I walked the half-mile to the station, stopping to chat with a friend along the way—her comment about my messy appearance made me laugh. The PATH station was filled with people headed to work and I had to push my way through the doors to squeeze in tightly before I let another train pass and be late for work.

I was good at my job. I found it easy, and convenient, considering I showed up hungover quite a bit. My boss treated me well and allowed me to take as much free time as I needed as long as the work was completed. I would spend the rest of the day scrolling my phone or going on a walk with my coworker Brandon. I jokingly forgave him for introducing me to Paul.

I couldn't explain why I didn't think of Brandon as more than a friend. He had been a listening ear through both the relationship and breakup with Jack, offering his advice, though often unsolicited, and we somehow formed a close bond, but it never drifted into romantic status. I felt oddly comfortable sharing the deep details of my current relationships with him, even though I kept my past to myself as I'd always done.

"I slept with Andrew last night," I divulged.

"I was wondering when that would finally happen," Brandon said. "You know you can never have a relationship with him now, right?"

"I already told you—I'm not looking for that," I said matter-of-factly, but then continued, skeptical. "But what do you mean?"

"You slept with him before you made him take you out on a date first. The sex is done, and he's not interested anymore. This is exactly what happened with Paul," Brandon said candidly. He didn't hold back from telling me exactly what he was thinking for the sake of hurting my feelings. He didn't know my vulnerability and thought I was stronger than I was. I put on a good front.

"Well, why should I have to make him take me out on a date?" I asked. "I can afford my own food."

"Yes, but men need the thrill of the chase," Brandon said.

"That sounds pretty ridiculous." I brushed him off, but deep down I was a little shaken by what he said. Though I had been entering into more superficial "situationships" for a few months now, this new way of life was still very new to me. I told myself and others that I wasn't looking for a deeper relationship, but inside I knew nothing different. It was a hard transition to this more casual lifestyle.

Back at my desk, Brandon's words stuck with me. *Was I just looking for a hookup, or did I want a more meaningful relationship, something I was more familiar with?* I reluctantly took the phone out of my bag and sent Andrew a text.

"I had fun last night. Hope you didn't rob me," I wrote, and then turned my phone to silent and placed it on the desk face down.

Half an hour later, I checked it. No response.

Another hour passed, and Andrew finally wrote back.

"Haha."

He was short with me, much shorter than the previous flirty texts we had shared before, and my motivation for going to the bar that night was evident. Andrew was often out for Monday night football and this was my chance to figure out if he truly was busy. But he never showed up and I was disappointed.

It took me a few minutes, but then it hit me—I had no obligation to Andrew whatsoever. We weren't exclusive; we weren't even dating. This new feeling that took over didn't make me feel sad or lonely. Rather, it made me feel good, great even. I could do whatever, speak to whoever I wanted and not hurt anyone in the process. I was tipsy and surrounded by friends and more than fifty other people who I had never met before. The boy with freckles standing beside me gave me a quick glance, and I offered my number without even asking his name.

A few days later, Brandon and I were out on our walk. "You seem happy," he said, taking a bite of his burger.

"Yeah, I took your advice," I started. "And I threw it out the window."

"Oh yeah? Look at you."

"Yeah, I'm having fun. There's nothing wrong with that right?" I asked, trying to understand if, in fact, there was something wrong with that. Though I didn't outwardly tell anyone who I was sleeping with, I couldn't help but feel like what I was doing was not appropriate. I never took advantage of anyone I slept with and made my intentions known from the start, but there was something about it that made me feel uneasy.

"No, not at all. There's such a stigma around women having sex, but I don't think anyone should feel ashamed. Men do it all the time," Brandon said. "Of course, only if you're not hurting anyone in the process."

"I hope you're right."

~

Between work during the week and hanging out with friends on the weekend, I found it difficult to visit my mother who still lived in Nutley, which was about thirty minutes outside Hoboken. The time I did find though, which was about a few hours once or twice a month, Sam would often join me, and we would instantly slip back to the late nineties when it was just the three of us.

"Have you met anyone yet, Michelle?" Mom asked not more than two minutes after I stepped foot inside the apartment.

Mom, Sam, and I gathered around the small dining table in Mom's now one-bedroom apartment that was located a few doors down from the two-bedroom she rented when Sam and I were still in college. The apartments looked identical except for the missing bedroom. Mom made lasagna, still my favorite.

"Mom, I think I've made the decision to freeze my eggs," I said.

"No honey, listen to me. You're only thirty—you'll meet someone. You're so pretty and smart," Mom responded. She wanted me to have a family, the life she thought I deserved.

"I understand that's what you want, but I just don't know if it's ever going to happen. And I want children one day." I had been single for over a year now, and I was enjoying my freedom.

"I think it's a great idea," Sam chimed in.

"You should think about this a little more. It is not the way God intended," Mom said. "I don't like it."

With that, I felt like I was being pushed into a sort of invisible wall. As it was when I was a teenager, I didn't like being told what to do.

"I've made my decision," I responded tersely.

"Don't worry, Mom," Sam said. "It's not a difficult procedure."

"It's just not natural!" Mom wouldn't let up.

"Mom, it's fine," I said.

"I just don't understand women these days," Mom said aloud to no one else but herself as she rose to walk to the kitchen with her dirty dish. Sam and I rolled our eyes as we looked at each other.

Four months later, I underwent the egg extraction at a local reproductive facility. Alone, I sat in the waiting room surrounded by couples undergoing IVF or other procedures to have children. Unlike every other patient I saw at this facility, there was no one there to hold my hand as I was given the anesthesia, the part that made me the most nervous, and no one there to help when I woke up after the hour-long sleep. I did it on my own, slowly learning how I could finally take control of my life.

Still bloated from my retrieval, and the ensuing ovarian hyper-stimulation syndrome that left me bedridden for three days, I walked through the front door of the apartment to Sam sitting on the couch with William, her boyfriend of seven months now. William was friendly and quiet, keeping mostly to himself, but there was something about their relationship that didn't quite mesh. It was obvious that Sam and William had been fighting and I was quick to notice Sam's angry demeanor as soon as I entered. I instinctively became protective, feeling that I needed to safeguard her.

"Hey Sam, are you okay?" I asked.

"Yeah, I'm fine," Sam responded curtly. William clenched his hands as he sat silently next to Sam.

"Can you give us a minute?" I asked William.

"I'll be outside," he said, forcing a smile, and stepped into the hallway.

"Thank you," I said to William. I closed the door and turned to Sam. "You're obviously upset. What happened?"

"It's really none of your business," Sam said.

"I live in this apartment, and I hear you two fighting all the time—he's always here."

"Just stop it!" Sam was angry.

"I'm not trying to fight, but I see you making the same mistakes I did. I'm trying to help."

"I'm not YOU," Sam snapped, and walked out the front door, slamming it behind her.

That moment was the beginning of a series of fights between me and Sam. She continued to date William, and we started clashing almost every day.

Though I didn't realize it then, it is now apparent to me that Sam and I had grown up living two completely different realities even though we resided in the same house. On one hand, Sam craved independence, wanting to make her own choices. On the other, having been given a parental role at such an early age, I was acting as a mother-figure, giving Sam advice that I expected her to follow as opposed to a sister, a confidant who would sit and listen. My upbringing allowed for nothing else.

Sam would fight like hell though. I tried talking to her pragmatically, patiently, but I would constantly get hit with her yelling at me. Looking back, I don't remember what we used to argue about, but I do recall her taking jabs at me, knowing exactly what would drive the knife deep.

"I'm moving out," she said to end our last fight.

I took a step back. "You're what?" It felt like I got punched in the gut.

"I'm not moving in with William, so get that out of your head," she said. "I've decided to move in with a friend downtown."

"When?"

"I'll give you a month to find someone new."

"Fine, maybe it's better this way," I said, not believing a word that came out of my mouth.

"It will be," she confirmed.

Sam, the only person who I thought would always be there for me, was pulling away.

Chapter 16
The Weight of What's Necessary

February 2014

Thanksgiving and Christmas were difficult for me that year because as much as Sam and I tried to hide the friction when we visited home, it was obvious Mom could sense we were drifting apart. Mom knew we were no longer living together, but I blamed it on wanting to meet new people. I not only felt the sting of slowly losing my sister, but also the guilt of it happening in front of our mother who once told me that Sam was the greatest gift she could ever give me. I felt a responsibility to keep it that way but instead, I was disappointing both myself and my mother.

Aside from this, Mom's bipolar had largely been controlled, with very few incidents over the past few years, and it seemed like she was finally in the clear. Mom seemed to enjoy her job, and the friends that came along with it, and even though she relied heavily on my monthly financial contribution, she seemed to be doing well enough to get by.

But then, just as I was about to breathe the proverbial sigh of relief, I was blindsided by my mother's unexpected decision to stop her medication.

It was now February 2014, and I was thirty-one years old. As soon as I walked through the front door of her apartment, it was clear that Mom required help. I had tried calling several times the night before and that morning, and when she didn't answer, I made the drive back home. Motionless, Mom stood like a statue in the living room with only a blank stare on her pale, sunken face. The television was turned to the local news in the background, but Mom stood nowhere near it and was obviously not paying attention. Instead, she was facing the white wall, glaring at its emptiness.

I usually called Mom once a day to check up on her even if it had been to listen to her babble on about how the neighbor had been pissing her off for blasting his music too loudly or complain about how she didn't have enough money for cigarettes. ("Mom, you're lucky you have food," I would remind her). But those past two weeks, I had been busy with work and friends and didn't have a chance to catch up with her. I immediately felt accountable.

"Mom," I sighed with regret. "Mom, did you take your medication?" I already knew the answer to my question.

"I'm fine."

"Mom, you're not fine. You're just staring at the wall," I said. "Please come over here."

"Okay. I'll just sit here," Mom said, sounding like a robot. She moved at a snail's pace to sit down on the couch next to me. When Mom stopped taking her medication, her mind would drift off, and it was impossible for her to hold a conversation.

Even though Sam and I were fighting, I knew I could reach out to her anytime it involved Mom.

"Listen, I can't really talk…" Sam started to say when she answered.

"I think we need to bring Mom to the hospital."

"Oh no. I'll be right there," Sam said without hesitation.

In less than an hour, Sam walked through the front door, and she too knew right away. "Yes, we definitely need to bring her to the hospital."

Then, as if a light bulb turned on when we accidentally said the word "hospital" too loudly, Mom perked up. By now, she knew Sam and I had control over her when making this decision and there was nothing she could do to stop it. This time she tried though, begging with all her might to change our minds.

"Girls, please no. Please don't bring me. I'm fine, I promise. I can't be in that place. I just can't. Girls, please."

I felt the deep guilt I was so accustomed to. "Mom, we love you so much. The doctors will help you. We don't know what else to do."

"Mommy, you'll be okay," Sam said.

Sam and I were sure from experience that Mom would be out in less than a month but making the choice to admit her was far from easy. My heart wrung with sadness, and it felt overpowering. I knew I had the choice to take time off from work and stop hanging out with friends to take care of her, and that choice left a feeling of remorse and shame because ultimately, I chose what was best for me, not what was best for Mom.

I took Sam into the kitchen, our differences aside for the moment. "We will bring her tomorrow. I'll stay the night," I said.

"Okay," Sam said. "I'll be back first thing tomorrow."

I spent the rest of the day and night with Mom, watching game shows and cooking dinner that neither of us ate. Mom barely spoke for the five hours we spent together before bedtime. Around ten at night, I took her into the bedroom and tucked her in, while I slept on the couch.

Shortly after midnight, I woke up startled. Like a ghost in the room, Mom was hovering over me, speechless. She didn't move; she just stared directly at me in the darkness. I was terrified and gasped, "Mom!" as she moaned in sorrow.

I let my guard down as I slowly realized what was happening. It was clear that she was in a state of delusion. "Oh Mom, come here." I took her hand and sat her down on the couch. "It'll be okay, I promise." I sat there with her for the rest of the night, a tear falling down my face every so often. The feeling of agony prevented me from sleeping, as my mother's head rested in my lap.

The next morning, Sam returned to Mom's apartment, and we gathered a few items of clothes and toiletries into a small overnight bag. Mom was still apprehensive but went into the car more willingly than I expected.

"Mom, we are going to bring you to Stonewall now. You'll be out in a few weeks," Sam reassured her. Surprisingly, Mom remained silent during the twenty-minute drive to the hospital.

Mom had been admitted to the Stonewall psychiatric unit numerous times before, but this time, the floor seemed eerily quiet, silent except for a random outburst from an inpatient every few minutes. The hallways lined with doors to each of the rooms were empty except for two or three other patients aimlessly pacing the floor with no one to guide them.

When I was younger, I feared this place mainly because movies and shows I'd seen over the years portrayed mental hospitals as these frightening scenes that housed menacing individuals. Now though, I realized my fear was due to a lack of understanding and as I walked through the halls with my mother, I knew there was no reason to be afraid. This wasn't a criminal institution and these men and women weren't dangerous; they just had a medical condition and required care.

As we escorted Mom to the administrative desk at the back end of the hallway, a woman, very obviously another patient, followed us. In the past, I would have called a nurse or walked faster to get away from the woman but this time, I stopped, turned around, and smiled genuinely. The woman smiled back with a glisten in her eye and skipped away gleefully.

"Hi, we'd like to check our mother in," I said to one of the nurses at the desk.

"I'm sorry, girls," the nurse responded sympathetically. She recognized us from previous visits. "We will take care of her. Janet, you can come with me." The nurse reached for Mom's hand.

As it has always been, leaving the hospital after visitation was the same draining experience. Mom slowly followed us like a pup whose owner was abandoning her, lingering closely behind until we reached the double doors that locked from the inside. There, the nurses held Mom back as she cried, begging us to take her home. I gave her a strong hug this time, but it didn't, as it never did, change the outcome.

"We love you, Mommy," Sam said. I gave a comforting smile

but choked up before I could let a word out. We turned around and walked out the door as my mother sobbed.

Sam and I visited Mom almost every other day. We would make our way to the common area where patients occupying the array of lounge chairs stared up at the television overhead, never moving. Sam or I would then escort Mom to the white-painted visitation room that was filled with tables and dining chairs, a dusty bookshelf, and a television playing some sort of sitcom. Given how often I visited, and how many patients were in the unit, I expected to see more visitors during the allotted visitation time, but there were usually only two or three other families in the room when I was there.

During this particular visit though, six other families were in the visitation room, and I was pleasantly surprised by the company. I found it easy to differentiate between patient and visitor simply by looking at their shoes. Mom wore a plain white shirt and slacks, her sneakers folded open, laces removed. It looked like she hadn't showered in a couple days as her gray roots were greasy along the hairline, but otherwise she looked like she was being cared for. She sat quietly between me and Sam, rarely making a sound other than a simple grunt every so often. For someone who spoke constantly for hours at a time over the phone, her lack of conversation was always strange to me.

"Hey Mom, how are you doing?" I asked.

"Eh," Mom muttered, looking around the room, not focusing on anything in particular.

"I had a good day at work. My boss was happy I finally handed in the research paper I was working on," I said, trying my best to make conversation.

"Okay," Mom said. She didn't quite sound angry, but I felt a subtle dig at me for making the decision to admit her to the hospital, almost as if she were punishing me.

"What did you have for dinner?" I asked, but Mom didn't answer. I kept talking though, never stopping the one-way conversation. I spoke about how I went on a date the night before, about my job, anything to keep my mother's spirits up and to make me feel less responsible for the way she was feeling. The one thing I would never talk about though was my father.

"It'll be okay, Mom," I said as I picked up my belongings and gave her a kiss as she, once again, followed me to the double doors.

Since Mom was admitted to the hospital, Sam and I started talking more than we had over the past four months. She ended her relationship with William about a month prior, and that somewhat helped to repair our relationship, but it seemed that commiserating about our mother made us each forget what we were fighting about. Only we could understand what the other was going through. The invisible air of discord between us evaporated.

In fact, I needed Sam, because when it came to my mother, I had few people I could talk to. The other options were Aunt Gail, Aunt Francine, or my father, and unfortunately discussing Mom with any of them caused stress, something I really didn't need.

For one, involving my aunts in discussions concerning Mom never ended well. Over the years, they increasingly wanted me to take on a more active role in my mother's care, but I knew whatever efforts I provided would be futile as Mom required full-time supervision. It didn't make me feel any less ashamed though and I decided to stay away as often as I could.

When it came to my father, my relationship with him improved, and we spoke almost weekly. Although we had our differences in the past, we didn't fight as much as we used to when I was younger, and I found that he was easy to talk to. We kept our conversation to more casual topics, like what was going on with my half-sisters or what projects kept me busy at work. We rarely spoke about my relationships though, and never about my mother.

Mom remained in Stonewall Hospital for a total of three weeks, at which point Doctor Lantire reached out to me. Mom had been under his care since my father introduced them twenty-five years ago.

"Hello? Is everything okay?" I asked. I knew there was something wrong since he was calling me directly.

"Hi, Michelle. As you are aware, your mother is not making any progress at Stonewall Hospital," Doctor Lantire said. "I believe you understand what the next steps are and I'm afraid it has come time to make a decision."

"Oh no," I replied, knowing full well what he was about to tell me. I had recalled this happening before, and although I was much younger the last time, I remembered it quite clearly.

Doctor Lantire continued. "Since she has shown no obvious signs of improvement, you need to decide if she will be cared for at home, or at Linden Hospital," he said. "Can you come in to meet with me today or tomorrow to discuss this?" Linden Hospital was a long-term inpatient facility for the mentally ill.

"I'll talk to my boss, but I'm sure there won't be a problem," I said. "I can be there around 4pm today. Does that work?"

"Yes, that's fine."

I rarely asked for time off, so my boss allowed me to leave early that day, no questions asked. Next, I called Sam.

"Hey," Sam said. She knew the news was not going to be good.

"Listen, I just spoke to the doctor. Mommy's not getting better. They want to move her to Linden Hospital."

"I had a feeling this was coming." Sam paused. "Why isn't she getting better? What happened?"

"I don't know. I'm at a loss. I hate this but I can't do it." I took a breath. "I can't be responsible if she doesn't get better. She needs to be under the care of medical professionals, not us." I thought about the guilt-trip I would receive from my aunts.

"I get it," Sam said. "And I completely agree." She somehow partially erased some of the regret looming over me.

"I'm headed over to the hospital soon," I said. "You can meet me there if you want, but I know you're working."

"I'll see what I can do, but I don't think I'll be able to leave today."

"It's fine. I can take care of it. I'll keep you posted."

Later that afternoon, I took the train back to Hoboken, walked the half mile back to my apartment, and got in my car. The bumper-to-bumper traffic along the highway made me anxious and I tried my best to keep my mind off the inevitable decision I would have to make.

The conference room was cramped so much so that Mom, Doctor Lantire, and I all sat within a couple feet of each other. I looked at my mother with sorrowful eyes, knowing she would hear and understand the conversation that I was about to have with the doctor, but also recognizing she would not say a word.

"Thank you for coming here so quickly," Doctor Lantire broke the silence. "Have you had a chance to think about what you want to do for your mother?"

"I have and honestly, I don't know what to do," I said, looking to my mother for any sort of guidance but getting none. "I don't want to admit her into Linden Hospital, but it seems like she will need 24/7 care. Is that right?"

"Yes, I don't think it would be in her best interest if she were left alone for an extended period of time," Doctor Lantire confirmed. He was gentle yet offered no other alternative.

"I know," I said, starting to feel the shame creep up inside me. Feeling like I had no other choice, I started rambling. "She wanders, often in the middle of the night. The Nutley police picked her up the last time she did that. She was in Belleville! Can you believe it? Belleville." I recalled the time Mom walked two miles to the neighboring town. "Anything she does at home—cooking, showering, getting dressed—it's a risk..."

Doctor Lantire stopped me from continuing. "You don't need to explain the situation to me. We understand completely," he said. "I would highly suggest she be taken in at Linden Hospital then." He quickly, but temporarily, brought me back down from my cloud of culpability, though the look on my mother's face after he spoke lifted me right back up again.

It didn't take much more than ten minutes, but I made the final decision that Linden Hospital was not only the best option. It was the only option.

Chapter 17

What Didn't Come Back

March 2014

Linden Hospital was smaller than Stonewall, but the entire building consisted solely of patients with psychiatric disorders. The front door leading into the facility opened to a large welcome area where the receptionist greeted visitors with a smile. It was the second reception area within the unit itself where nurses and staff were more hostile.

Down a long hallway, much like the one at Stonewall, gold plaques commemorating renowned doctors and founders of the hospital lined the corridor. At the end of the hallway there was a conference room to the right, and to the left, a set of locked doors that could only be opened by a designated worker. These doors led to the elevators which would bring visitors to either the second or third floor of the building. The second floor was where patients without criminal histories would be housed and where my mother would be staying. It was the third floor we wanted to stay away from.

The scent of disinfectant spray that wafted through the hallways was always so pungent. Sam and I, along with the guard, escorted Mom up the elevators to her new room at Linden Hospital. The second-floor unit was a dreary area filled with seriously ill patients, ranging in age from early twenties to late sixties, wandering the hallways seemingly loaded up on medication or sleeping in their beds. There were two expansive gathering areas where groups of patients would spend their time in therapy or working on mundane activities or crafts; coloring was this Wednesday night's entertainment. Mom's room was of course white. No flowers or cards were allowed in to brighten up the space.

"Mom, the room isn't too bad right?" I said, trying to make myself feel better.

"Yeah, look over here. The sheets are blue, your favorite color," Sam added.

Mom trudged to her bed and lay down, pulling the covers over her body like a frightened child. Sam and I sat next to her for a few minutes but without knowing what to do or say, we gave her a kiss on the forehead and let her be.

I made time to see Mom at least once a weekend. I was allowed to take her out of the facility for a few hours at a time if I signed a release form agreeing to bring her back by the end of the day. I made it a point to take her out whenever I could even if it was only to run an errand or grab a slice of pizza.

Three months went by, and I started to notice that Mom was improving. I didn't think she was at the point where she could be discharged from the hospital, but it seemed like she was headed in the right direction.

The following week, I decided to take her out to a local diner for lunch.

"Isn't this place great?" I asked her.

"Yes, I like it," she said, looking at the pictures of celebrities hung up on the walls. Mom wasn't talking much, but I was able to at least elicit some sort of conversation. She seemed a little spaced-out, disoriented, but I didn't think anything of it, and attributed it to her just having a bad day.

A few minutes later, we received the menus. "What do you want to eat?" I asked as I perused the one I was given.

"My stomach hurts. I don't want to eat," she said as she rubbed her abdomen with a pained look on her face

I put the menu down on the table. "Are you okay?"

"No."

"Do you want to see a doctor?"

"Yes."

I didn't even think; I exited the booth and put my hand on her arm, slowly leading her out to the car. I took her to Doctor Pret, our general physician who was located five minutes from the diner. He was Mom's medical doctor, and Sam and I had been going to him since we were teenagers—I trusted him completely. He was genuine, calm, and extremely smart. By the time we reached his office, I noticed my mother was more confused than I realized, and I knew something was wrong.

Doctor Pret examined my mother and requested a urine sample. Unfortunately, Mom was unable to give one in her absent-minded condition and there was no way I could help. Without a urine sample to test, Doctor Pret could not diagnose her condition but told me that I made the right decision bringing her in, and I should inform the doctors at Linden Hospital right away.

I thanked Doctor Pret and brought her back to Linden. There, I explained how she had been acting while we were out, and one of the nurses said they would examine her. I wanted to stay but was asked to leave because visiting hours were over.

Over the next few days, Mom continued to complain about stomach pains and her muddled expressions seemed to worsen. When I followed up with the doctor, I was told Mom had a urinary tract infection and was given anti-bacterial medication. This seemed to address her stomach pains, not so much the disorientation, but I decided to put my confidence into the medical staff at Linden Hospital.

The following weekend, I returned to see Mom. It was raining hard outside and I found it difficult to drive through the streets as the sun was setting. Because of this, I showed up late, toward the end of the visiting hour. The bottom of my pants was soaked as I trudged down the long hallway and up the elevator to my mother's unit. I signed in and requested to see her.

"Your mother is being restrained," a nurse said, holding a clipboard in hand. "You are unable to see her right now."

"What do you mean, she is being restrained?" I asked, utterly confused. I was already on edge about my mother and felt the pang of anger coming to the surface.

"I don't have that information," she said. "I believe they are performing blood tests."

"Why do they need to restrain her to take blood tests?" I asked. "I would like to see her now."

"I will bring her out when I can."

I took a seat on a bench in the entry room. One hour later, my mother emerged, shaking uncontrollably, and it was to the point where I was now scared. I ran up to her and gave her a hug, but she couldn't stop trembling and looked terrified, her eyes wide with fear.

"We need to bring her to a medical hospital immediately!" I shouted.

"Unfortunately, we cannot bring her to a medical hospital unless her fever is over 103 degrees," the nurse said. "But don't worry, the medical doctor here is fully capable."

"Why is she shaking like this?" I asked, scared for her.

"She is on antibiotics for her urinary tract infection," she said.

"That doesn't make any sense."

"I'm sorry but there is nothing else we can do at this time."

"I want to see the results of the blood test."

"We don't have them right now, but you can call in a couple hours for the results."

I didn't know what else to do. I felt panicky, and downright troubled about how they were handling my mother's care. I thought about taking her home myself, but that thought was fleeting considering, one, I had no idea what was going on with her, and two, I had no one to watch her during the day while I was at work. I was forced to leave her in the care of the hospital.

I gave my mother a long hug and whispered "I'm so sorry, Mom" in her ear. Then I turned around and walked out the door.

When I arrived back at the apartment that night, I reached out to the hospital. "Hi, I'm calling for the blood tests results for my mother, Janet Hanes," I said. "I was told they would be ready by now."

"Oh, I'm sorry, we cannot give you that information over the phone," the nurse had the nerve to tell me. "You will need to come in and request a copy here."

"No," I said. "I was told the results would be given to me over the phone."

"I'm sorry, we cannot do that."

"Can you at least tell me if there is anything I need to worry about? If what my mother has is serious?"

"From what the doctor told me, it is not serious."

That reassurance did not hold up however. I found out the next day, when I asked to speak with the doctor directly, that my mother was admitted to the emergency room at Stonewall Hospital that night.

"I was told yesterday, very clearly by the nurse, that my mother's condition was not serious," I told Doctor Yemseh, the medical doctor in charge of her care at Linden Hospital. "Today, I found out she was admitted to the emergency room at Stonewall and is still there."

"We brought her to the hospital for lithium toxicity," he said. "However, this is nothing serious, and she should return in a day or two." Doctor Yemseh was direct, but also seemed oddly unconcerned, almost as if he had something more important to attend to.

The word "toxicity" sounded very serious though. Doctor Yemseh had been so vague, as if there was nothing wrong and no more questions needed to be asked. But questions were the only thing forming in my mind, and all I could do was point my finger at myself for whatever predicament Mom was in. Just a few short weeks before I admitted her to Stonewall Hospital, she was her normal self. Now that she was residing in Linden Hospital, her condition had unexpectedly worsened to the point where I was now fearful.

I wouldn't let Doctor Yemseh brush me off. "I don't understand why you are saying this is nothing serious. I spoke with the doctor at Stonewall Hospital who told me this was in fact, very serious, and her lithium levels should have been tracked very closely," I retorted.

"We do track her lithium levels very closely and there is nothing else we can do," he said. "I'm sorry to cut you off, but I need to attend to a patient." He hung up the phone before I could say another word.

I reeled at the phone in disbelief.

The next night, I met up with Sam at Linden Hospital. We walked down the hallway lined with plaques, past the front desk without signing in, and right into Mom's room.

"Hi, Mom," Sam and I both said at the same time.

Mom grunted. Although she had been conversational just a few days ago, even if only slightly, she barely spoke today. She sat beside us in silence glaring off into the distance.

"We're going to get you out of here," I told her. "We just need to figure out a few things first, but you won't be here much longer, I promise." Mom then looked at me, her eyes hopeful.

When the visitation hour was up, Sam and I kissed our mother goodbye and walked to the parking lot. Under the light of the lamppost, Sam and I discussed next steps.

"I know you don't want to hear this, but maybe we should ask Aunt Francine and Aunt Gail to come with us next time," Sam said.

"I don't think we have a choice," I responded. I got into my car and started to pull away. "I'm going to schedule a meeting with the doctor next Thursday at 7pm for all of us. Can you make it?"

"I'll be there."

"Thanks," I said as I drove away alone into the night.

Behind the wheel of my small two-wheel drive sedan, I veered around a corner and almost skid off the road when a squirrel ran in front of the car. I pulled off to the side of the road, scared.

Then, I screamed.

~

The week passed with minimal incident, and I spent the time thinking of possible solutions. I came up with nothing. When Thursday came, seven people gathered around the large conference table at Linden Hospital—me, Sam, Aunt Francine, Aunt Gail, Uncle Larry, who decided to join last minute, a nurse, and Doctor Yemseh.

I started speaking and tried my best to keep my composure even though I felt completely overwhelmed. "Doctor Yemseh, we want to take our mother home. What can you tell us about her condition?"

"As you know, Janet has been here for four months. We are starting to see slight improvement, but it is minimal and she still requires full time care, at least for the time being," he explained.

"Can you tell us what happened last week?" I asked. "We were told by one of the nurses that she was given too much of her lithium medication." I was trying with all my might not to shout at him.

"Uh, well, she was given too much of that medication, yes, but it hasn't affected her health negatively in any way," Doctor Yemseh said. To me, he didn't sound too sure of himself.

"We understand she needs full-time care, and we don't know what to do. What are our options?" Sam asked.

"Well, you could take her in," Aunt Gail said stiffly from the other side of the table.

"You could take her in too, Aunt Gail," Sam shot back.

"We understand this is difficult," Doctor Yemseh interrupted. "The only way we can release her is if we have a guarantee from someone that she will be under someone's care."

Then out of nowhere, Uncle Larry spoke. "I can do it."

Six pairs of eyes looked over at him, stunned. Not one person in the room was expecting him to speak, no less offer to take Mom in. Uncle Larry was Mom's younger, quieter brother and didn't often get involved in her care, but he rented his own space and was no longer working so he had the capacity to care for her during the week.

The doctor scoured the room for any hint of opposition, and when he received none, he continued speaking. "Okay I can go over the medication protocol with you, Larry. It appears everyone agrees, so we should be all set," Doctor Yemseh said.

"Are you sure about this, Larry?" Aunt Francine asked.

"Yes. I think everyone agrees she can't stay here much longer," he said.

My aunts nodded; I dropped my head down into my chest and noticed out of the corner of my eye, Sam did the same. I felt insecure and skeptical about the decision. I wasn't that close with Uncle Larry, but I was unable to come up with any other solution and knew my uncle well enough to think he was at least capable of what was being offered. I felt selfish though, not willing to give up my life the way I had when I was a teenager. I had thought of ways Mom could live with me but realized how drastically it would upend my life. I was technically single, but still dating, and all that would end in an instant. And even if I didn't fully trust I would settle down again, I didn't completely give up hope.

Hiring a caregiver so Mom could return to her apartment alone was the only other option, but at the private rate of twenty dollars an hour it was financially impossible. I made decent money, but it was only enough to cover my necessities, a couple nights out a week, and the money I gave to Mom each month for food and essentials, while still having some money leftover to put into savings. Plus, I didn't want Mom to spend one more second than she had to in Linden Hospital. I went along with the only feasible plan.

~

The day she was released, Sam and I held Mom's hands as she walked through the double doors that were locked from the inside and out to my car. The summer sun was shining, and it was beautifully warm as she looked up at the clouds with, what seemed to me, both a feeling of freedom and a yearning for something more, something better. The drive to Uncle Larry's apartment took less than fifteen minutes but I noticed Mom smile for the first time in almost six months. Sam and I hugged her goodbye, both happy that she was no longer bound by the confines of the hospital and worried about what her future held.

It took a mere five days, less than a full week, after Mom moved in with her brother that he thoroughly relinquished all responsibility. According to Uncle Larry, my mother was "too codependent" and he needed his freedom. He packed up Mom's belongings and moved her back into her apartment without looking back. Neither Sam nor I was informed of his decision, and I only found out when I stopped by my mother's apartment a few days later to check in on it.

"Mom! What are you doing here alone?" I asked after finding her in the bedroom. I had heard a noise and searched the apartment nervously, hoping she wasn't being robbed.

"It's nice being home, honey," Mom responded. I felt relieved that she was finally talking again.

Though I harbored anger toward my uncle for being so dismissive, Sam and I found that Mom's mental health improved being in her home environment. Mom had not healed to the point where she could care for herself and though her safety was still in question, she became more conversational. She was alone though so I made it a priority to call at least once a day and visit more often, at least once every two weeks even if it was only for an hour.

Even though my mother was better than she was while in the hospital, she wasn't completely back to her normal self. During each visit, I tried to assess her level of competency to see if she could effectively care for herself, but I only saw minor improvement since she had first arrived at her apartment from the hospital two months ago.

"Hey, Mom," I said one Saturday afternoon.

She was drying a small dish in the kitchen, towel in hand. She turned to see me, smiling. "Hey, honey," she said. I noticed right away that she spoke more slowly than normal. "What do you want for dinner?"

"Oh, I'm sorry, Mom, I can't stay for dinner. But I wanted to stop by and say hi," I explained.

"Really?" Mom said. It was clear to me she didn't want me to leave from the tone of that single word.

"I'm sorry. Next time, I promise."

"That's okay. Can you put this dish away? I can't reach." Mom stretched her arms up to the top shelf of the cabinet.

"Sure," I said.

"Hey, what do you want for dinner?" Mom asked a second time.

I was now concerned. "Mom, you already asked that. And I just told you I couldn't stay."

"Did I?"

"Yes," I said and then paused for a moment noticing her demeanor. "Are you okay?"

"Umm…" Mom was trembling nervously. "Where was that dish I was washing?"

"Mom?" I asked, walking over to her. With a gentle touch, I put my hand on her arm and led her to the dining room table where we sat down next to each other. Mom slowly started to stop shaking as she looked at me. She didn't speak for a few moments. Then as she stopped shuddering, she picked my hand up and held it in hers as the sadness in her eyes burned straight through me.

"Michelle, I think there's something wrong."

It was then that it registered—the moment I realized I had lost my mom. It wasn't that she was physically gone; it was that the mom I had just a few months ago was gone. The mom I could talk for hours on the phone with or banter back and forth with or cry with when I broke up with a boyfriend. The mom who would never come back to me.

"Hey, Mom, you're okay. You're okay, I promise. I'm here." I hugged her tightly, as tightly as I hugged Sam, and as tightly as I hugged Dad all those years ago. I stayed with my mom until she calmed. Then she smiled and looked at me.

"I love you, my Michelle," she said. It seemed as if she had forgotten why she was shaking.

"I love you too, Mom. Are you okay?"

"Yes, I'm okay. You should go."

I gave her one more hug, told her I loved her, and then I walked out the door.

I had to live my life, but my mom still needed me. She needed me as much as I needed her when I had my first breakup or when I had my first panic attack or when I was simply just sad. But that night, I walked away.

Chapter 18

The Face Behind the Mask

August 2015

Mom was only sixty years old when she was diagnosed with Alzheimer's. This, along with a second diagnosis of aphasia, slowly took her over the next few months. Mom's initial realization was the beginning of yet another years-long disease and new kind of suffering for someone who had undergone so much pain and loss already. After she was formally diagnosed, she had to quit her waitressing job that she held on to for so many years, the one that she loved so much, and the one that kept her from spiraling.

Her memory was fading, but at least I could still talk to her. Before her diagnosis, Mom and I would speak multiple times a week and I would get bored at the same topics day in and day out, letting my mother talk without adding much to the conversation. These past months though, I would talk quite a bit, often more than her, telling stories of when Sam and I were children, just enough to make her smile. And just enough to make me cry.

By August 2015, nine months after her diagnosis, Mom was barely able to form a full sentence. Her lack of communication concerned me, but I was stuck, not knowing exactly what to do to help. In addition to the communication difficulties, Mom could no longer leave the house without being sure that she turned the stove off, nor could she put on a full outfit independently—she could get her undergarments on, but a shirt or pants proved troublesome. She also used to walk to the main street in town a few blocks from the apartment to get her nails done, but now she was getting lost on the multiple side streets on the way to the salon.

I decided she needed an in-home caregiver, yet I had no idea where to start. My mother had no savings, so hiring a private aide was not possible. I decided to look further into her insurance, and found that, with an Alzheimer's diagnosis, both her Medicare and Medicaid would cover the full cost of an at-home aide for at least part of the day.

Though the caretaker was fully covered by insurance, the process was cumbersome and involved months of interviews and filling out paperwork. Questions like "can the patient dress herself," or "can the patient prepare meals for herself," littered the pages. I found myself answering "no" to all of them. On top of that, I would spend hours on the phone trying to contact anyone who could help or move the process along. It was frustrating, and I resented the amount of time I had to spend on getting my mother, someone who desperately needed it, care. Eventually, Mom was assigned a health advocate who was able to work with me.

The results of the multitude of surveys and questionnaires showed that Mom would receive the maximum allowed hours of care. This amounted to eight hours a day on weekdays—nine in the morning to five at night, Monday through Friday. It was the other sixteen hours in the day, and weekends, that proved difficult. I had wondered, after spending countless hours trying to find an aide, if a nursing home would be the better choice.

The caregiver I hired was well equipped to meet Mom's needs. Rosa, a short, stocky middle-aged woman, was kind and resourceful, but her first language was not English. This made it difficult to coordinate weekly schedules that seemed to change quite a bit with doctor's appointments and visits from family, but overall things progressed well under her care. Rosa's lack of the English language didn't seem to bother Mom though. Mom couldn't speak much, but I assume not having to communicate at all with her new live-in aide made residing with a stranger more bearable.

During this time, Mom received government approval to move into Section 8 housing in the neighboring town. Since she was no longer able to work, it would have been impossible otherwise to afford her Nutley apartment. I had helped her apply several years ago for housing assistance, but it was not until two months after she was diagnosed with dementia and aphasia that she was approved.

In addition to the stress of relocating my mother and finding her care, I had been drinking quite a bit since I moved to Hoboken three years prior. I also found myself dating a different guy every two weeks. It wasn't that my mother's illness impacted my choices, it was more that the dating scene had become too difficult, fleeting. Dating apps were now a thing and it seemed like everyone, including myself, could always find someone better. I'd spend the night with someone, and we'd talk for a week or two, but then he or I would get bored and find someone else to do the same with.

I told myself I was taking control, but deep down, after the initial sense of freedom wore off, all I felt was loneliness.

I started to question if what I really wanted was to be alone. *Did I want to make my own decisions without having to worry about what anyone else thought? Or did I want to be with someone and then essentially lose a part of myself, the part that allowed me to do what I wanted, when I wanted?*

My desire for attachment was at the same time, counteracted by my fear of it. It was strange since only a few years prior, I couldn't imagine myself *not* being in a relationship. But now, once I received the attention I craved, be it from someone who truly wanted to start a long-term relationship with me or just in general, I would pull away, sparing myself the hurt I knew all too well. I was being pulled in two completely opposite directions and couldn't figure out what would truly make me happy.

I was crashing, suddenly realizing how truly alone I was, and at the same time, losing all sense of self. I questioned almost everything in my life since I was a child, but they mostly centered around one of two events: my parents' divorce and the sexual assault at Oak Beach. *Was I primed as a child to act this way as an adult? Is this what I was meant to become? Did sexual abuse affect how I approached every relationship I've ever been in?*

Was I enough?

~

"Would you like another?"

I lifted my head up from my phone. The man who approached me from behind was quintessentially tall, dark, and handsome. But he didn't look like the other men I had been dating; instead, he displayed a slight eeriness that intrigued me.

"I would," I said with a smile.

"Why are you drinking by yourself at this hole in the wall?" he asked.

I wasn't at my usual spot. I felt an urge to get out of the apartment and instead of walking the half-mile down to The Factory, I stopped by the dive bar about fifty feet down the street from my apartment, a place that rarely served more than a few patrons at a time, especially on a Tuesday night. Before he approached me, I was alone, scrolling on my phone and exchanging a few words with the bartender. It was dark and the music low, and there seemed to be a slight fogginess in the atmosphere, though I wasn't sure where it came from.

"I don't mind it here," I said. "It's eclectic."

"What's your name?"

"Michelle."

"I'm Drew. Nice to meet you."

Drew sat down beside me on a barstool and ordered two drinks: a vodka tonic for himself and a beer, my drink of choice. From what I could tell, he was the complete opposite of me, seemingly untroubled by anything, but somehow, we clicked immediately. We shared stories of past relationships and what we thought our futures held. By the end of the night, we were the only two people at the bar, my girlish giggles filling the silence as the music turned off and the lights came on.

"Do you want to get out of here?" I asked.

"Let's go to my place."

Drew's place was well-kept, almost pristine. He owned a two-bedroom apartment that overlooked the Hudson River in the more upscale part of Hoboken. The whole apartment was bright and airy, and the spacious living room boasted floor to ceiling windows and opened up to the all-white kitchen. The two bedrooms overlooked the city, and each had a walk-in closet. Drew and I spent another hour drinking wine and listening to the low ambient music that filled the apartment.

What usually ended as a one-night stand turned into months of dates, couch cuddles, and, most importantly, a sense of trust, something I hadn't felt in a few years. I was finally entering into a relationship with someone I could rely on. I was living a dream and falling for the man I met at the dive bar.

"Do you want to come by my place tonight?" Drew texted me one day after work. "I'll cook and you can relax."

"Be there at seven," I wrote.

That night, I tapped on the door and peeked my head in as I pushed it open. Drew was bustling about the kitchen, running between the oven and the stove, stirring whatever was in the pot. He removed his oven mitts and met me at the door to give me a kiss on the forehead.

"It's almost ready. I'm just slicing some veggies for the salad and we can eat!" Drew was excited, and I was beside myself seeing a man working so hard to please me. He had been like this since we met, and I was starting to get used to it.

"Thank you for all of this," I said shyly. "Here, I brought something." I handed him the six pack.

"Light beer, huh? You couldn't have grabbed a Pilsner?" He was joking but I noticed a hint of harshness. I paused for a moment, surprised by the inconspicuous jab, but brushed it off and walked over to the dining table.

"It smells delicious."

"I made your favorite. The lasagna I make isn't the typical recipe," Drew said. "Here, try this sauce." He cooled off the sauce with a blow and brought the wooden spoon to my mouth.

"This is amazing," I gasped. "Seriously, this is the best sauce I've ever tasted."

"It was my sister's recipe," Drew said. "These are the little reminders that get me through the day."

"She lives on in your heart," I said sympathetically. When Drew told me about the way his sister endured three years of cancer before succumbing to the disease, I sunk into his arms offering whatever support I could.

The rest of the night went beautifully, just as I imagined it would. I felt comfortable confiding in Drew about the struggles with my mother, and he was able to talk to me about not only the loss of his sister but his own family hostilities. I was finally letting my guard down.

The next day at work, as I daydreamed about our night, I was caught off guard by my client. I had recently started a new job as a consultant, and my current boss was more conservative than my previous one. This was also my first assignment in this business line and though I received nothing but praise, I felt less confident in my work than when I was an analyst.

"Michelle, can you come to my office, please?" Evelyn asked in a stern voice. Evelyn was a tall, thin woman with a presence that powered over the entire office.

"Sure," I said from my desk outside her office.

I sat down slowly in the leather chair across from her desk and anxiously admired the view of downtown New York.

"Is everything okay?" I said, knowing something was wrong and wanting to get straight to the point.

"I noticed you've been leaving fifteen minutes early for the past few weeks and coming in after 9am," Evelyn said. "The work-day starts at 9am and ends at 5pm. If this continues, I will take action."

With that, I felt my nerves tense up, though I couldn't understand why my boss was being so strict about this. I didn't dare question her though. "Oh, uh, yes, I understand. I won't do it again."

"Thank you. That is all," Evelyn said, dismissing me. I walked out like a dog with a tail between her legs.

Back at my desk, I sat down and continued working briefly before a text from Drew caused my phone to light up, displaying the photo he and I took while walking along the river a few weeks prior.

"How's work?" the text read.

"Fine. Hey, I miss you and was hoping we could hang tonight," I said, replaying the conversation with my boss in my mind, hoping Drew could provide some sort of comfort.

"I would but I'm at the airport," he said. "I have to leave the state for a week."

"Oh, where are you going?" I asked, caught off guard that he was suddenly leaving.

"I have to go to Chicago for work."

"Wow, okay," I said. I was just with him and there was no mention of a work trip. "Will you text me when you get there?"

"I won't have access to my phone while I'm gone, but I'll try to text you when I can," he said.

I was not only confused but also felt a sudden loss of confidence in our relationship. *Why couldn't he text me while he was away?* I put down my phone on the desk and thought carefully before writing anything. Our relationship was still new, so I didn't want to come off too bold and push him away, but I wanted to know more.

"That's odd. Why can't you text me?" I asked.

"I have an important presentation and will be focusing on that while I'm away."

"I see. Okay, good luck," I wrote.

"Thanks, we can make plans when I get back. Sound good?"

I had a strange feeling but tried not to overthink it, though that was easier said than done.

"Sure."

A few days went by, and Drew and I did not exchange any texts. This was strange to me considering we had talked almost every day up until this point.

A week later, on the dot, Drew texted me and we made plans to hang out. I agreed to meet him at his place.

"How was your trip?" I asked when I walked through the door.

"Fine," Drew said tersely. "How was your week?"

"Not bad. I got a lot done at work and finally handed in that project I was working on." I put my coat on the chair near the entry.

"It's about time you handed that in. You've been working on it for almost a month." Something in Drew's voice sounded distant.

"I feel relieved," I said. "So, what do you want to do tonight?"

"Whatever you want."

I was used to Drew taking control and planning the evenings we spent together. This time was different though; he was cold toward me.

I planned to spend the night at his apartment, but his kisses felt forced, his hugs shallow, and I knew something was wrong. Instead of asking him directly though, I asked if I could stay. I figured I would get my answer that way.

"Um, not tonight. I have an early meeting tomorrow and it's getting late," Drew said. "Do you want me to drive you back?"

"No, I'll call a cab."

I walked out the front door feeling vulnerable, a sensation I hadn't faced in a while since I had been avoiding it for years. It hit me like a brick though and I receded into my own anxiety. The eight-minute cab ride downtown was silent. Usually I would, at a minimum, ask the driver how his day was. This time though, I didn't want to speak.

I was confused. *We didn't break up, so why was I so worried?* I decided I would hold on to whatever Drew and I had together and not question anything yet.

Over the next few weeks, our relationship, strangely enough, reverted mostly back to normal and I chalked his strange attitude up to a bad day.

But then a month later, Drew disappeared for another week, and this time, I didn't receive a text or call letting me know he was leaving, nor any responses to my texts. I decided to go to his place to find out what was going on. I rang the bell to his apartment, but there was no answer. I wasn't ready to leave so I sat on the steps outside his complex. A few minutes later, he opened the door.

"What are you doing here?" Drew asked, sounding frustrated.

"Where have you been?"

"I went away again for work," Drew replied, angry that I was there, invading on his privacy.

"Okay. Well, you could have just texted me, right?" Now I was angry.

"It was a last-minute trip. Why are you so mad?" he asked, starting to place the blame for this fight on me.

"I've been texting you all week with no response."

"What is your problem? I just went away for work for a few days and now I'm back. Stop grilling me," Drew said sharply.

The way he spoke, I actually started to question my anger. I paused and then continued, gaining the courage to ask my question. "Is there something wrong?"

"No," Drew said with questioning eyes. "What do you mean?"

I started to get defensive. "I don't know. It's just weird that you up and left without saying anything and come back and act like nothing's wrong."

"Listen, if you're going to act like this, I don't think we should be dating," Drew said. "I didn't do anything wrong."

"What are you talking about?"

"It really sounds like you're accusing me of something," Drew said.

The anger vanished and I was now getting upset. "No, I'm not. You're just acting strange and I don't know why," I said.

"I think you should just leave," Drew said. "I deserve better than how you are treating me."

His words struck me, and my short step back came on like a reflex. I was no longer upset, no longer angry; I was shocked. I stood up and walked down the block without saying goodbye.

I was able to hold my composure for most of the walk home until I broke down crying a block away from my apartment. *How could I have been so stupid?* I gave myself for months to this man I barely even knew. I did absolutely nothing wrong, but instead of feeling guilty and pointing the finger at myself like I had always done, I took a moment to think, to understand what happened.

He manipulated me.

I never found out where Drew went nor what he did while he was away, but at this point, it didn't matter because I no longer cared.

I walked up the stairs to my apartment, put my bag down on the kitchen table and walked into my bedroom. There, I looked into the mirror, staring at the black mascara running down my face and the pink lipstick smeared slightly along my cheek. I realized my strong will for connection had been offset by my utter naivety as I spent the last twenty years relying on other people to define my self-worth and neglected to focus on what truly made me happy.

I took a wet cloth and wiped off my mask. The face looking back at me was one I didn't recognize. It was better; it was one that exuded confidence and dignity. I looked directly at myself and said, "*I* deserve better."

Chapter 19
Written by My Own Hand

July 2016

"Writing is therapeutic."

My mother told me this a long time ago. When I was a child, I purchased a diary and wrote in it often but as I grew older, and my time became more limited, I put the diary aside and hadn't looked at it in years.

The large cardboard box kept hidden away in the closet at my mother's apartment was an emotional cluster of old memories. In it, I found pictures of the family before the divorce: Sam and I dressed up as princesses smiling happily, Dad with his arms wrapped around Mom, and pictures of Max cuddled up next to me as I was fast asleep. I held the pictures in my hand, smiling as I reminisced, yet sad thinking about what could have been.

After digging through more pictures, I found the pastel pink and purple diary with a small silver lock. It was broken as I had lost the key long ago. I opened it up and began reading. The first entry was about Matt, my first crush. Little hearts floated across the page with his name written in each one. The next few pages were about Oliver—how I fell for him the moment I saw him and how I felt betrayed when he cheated on me. Trevor took up the second half of the diary, but it ended abruptly after that. There was no mention of Ian.

I hadn't read my diary in more than fifteen years and as I skimmed through some of the entries, I saw how much I learned from when I was younger, how much I had grown. But with that, I also felt a sense of comfort knowing that although I couldn't change the past, my future had not yet been written.

I brought the entire box home to the apartment with me and placed it under my bed. I picked up the new leather-bound journal I received in the mail a few days ago and began to write. I wrote about everything from my family's past to my dating life to all the dogs I've loved. I didn't hold back and made sure to get everything out on the page, including the details about the assault at Oak Beach. Some things I shared with the rest of the world through the blog I started after Drew and I broke up, but most I kept to myself. It didn't matter though—just getting it all out onto the page felt cathartic, a way for me to get things off my chest. Instead of running away from my feelings, I was able to at least begin to organize the thoughts that ran rampant in my head. Writing became my outlet, my therapy.

~

It was a warm, clear summer afternoon in Hoboken. It had been almost a year since I hired a caregiver for my mother and even though it took a while, I finally relinquished the guilt of doing so;

rather, I felt relieved knowing she was safe. Drew was long forgotten and since the last time we spoke three months prior, I held my head high, making better decisions for myself when it came to dating. Things weren't perfect, but I found that writing in my journal was helping me to channel my emotions more productively.

I walked into The Factory and saw Bella hanging out at the bar. I sidled up next to her and ordered a beer, smiling in her direction. "Hey," I said nonchalantly and pulled the barstool out.

"Hey you! We haven't seen you here in a while," Bella said. "Where have you been?"

"Just taking a little time off. But I'm back for the time being."

"You know, I never liked Drew." Bella insinuated she knew the reason I wasn't around much.

"I don't think anyone did," I said, looking around. "Where is everyone?"

"A lot of the guys went golfing today, but they should be here soon. Have you met Seth?"

Seth peeked his head out from behind her back and introduced himself. He reached his hand out.

"I don't think I have," I said, shaking his hand.

"You're Michelle, right?"

"Yes. You must be new." I admired his blue eyes and kindhearted smile.

"Ha, I was dating someone, so I haven't been around in a while, but I've known Bella since high school."

"Yeah, he's a good one," Bella said, sounding genuine.

"That's what they all say." I gave them both a sly grin.

Seth, Bella, and I talked for a bit, but after a couple drinks, I went my separate way and walked home.

On the way, I stopped for a slice of pizza and sat at the outdoor table to observe whoever passed by. I saw a man stumbling home, chuckling to myself as I thought about the many times I had done the same. I saw a couple holding hands, kissing happily as they leaned into each other and wondered if that was ever meant for me. Then I saw a woman walking a small Yorkshire terrier and thought of Gizmo. Although I visited him once a month, the decision to re-home him years ago was difficult. My little pup wasn't happy without other dogs in his life. I smiled, thinking that he runs joyfully with his new friend and forgave myself for my choice.

The sun started to set beyond the horizon and the hot pink sky lit up the New York City skyline from across the river. I finished my slice of pizza, ordered a couple of garlic knots to go, and began my walk back to the apartment.

Along the way, I found a homeless woman sitting on the sidewalk cradling a small, skinny dog in her lap. Her clothes had holes in them, and she was wearing a knit hat. I looked over at her and gave her a faint grin. She saw me, and as if she didn't want to acknowledge anything else in her life, she started yelling, "Get away from me! Get away from my dog! Go away!" Rather than feeling scared, I felt like I could sense her loneliness. I took a step closer, calmly placing the garlic knots down at her side. Her dog sniffed the container and started wagging his tail.

And the woman smiled.

Back at the apartment, I opened my computer to write. The blog was getting popular and even though it was entirely comedic, I found it healing. I spent the next hour typing, but then my eyelids grew heavy, and I closed my laptop. The next morning, after a good night's sleep, I re-opened my blog to begin writing. My phone pinged.

"Hey, I hope you don't mind, but I got your number from Bella," Seth wrote. "I was wondering if you would want to grab a drink with me at the Pier later."

"Sure," I said.

Our first date went well, and then our second, and then our third. Seth treated me unlike Drew, or Oliver, or Jack, or Ian, or any of the other men I met while in Hoboken—he treated me the way I should have been treated for years. Our relationship didn't last one night or even a few months. Two years of dating turned into a beautiful marriage, one of genuine trust and stability, quite different from any I had in the past. I finally felt safe.

~

Over the years, I formed a new relationship with Dad and Jillian as well. The anger and resentment that I was never able to discuss with either of them formed like a giant bubble inside me that could never burst, and eventually it became too much for me to handle. So, one year before my wedding with Seth, I reached out to my father and asked him to join me for dinner, just the two of us.

We met at the local tavern and took a seat at one of the tables away from the entrance. Waiters and waitresses were bustling about taking orders, but other than that, it was a quiet, laid-back atmosphere, something both my father and I preferred. The lights were low, and I ordered water and my father, a soda.

"You know, this is the first time we have been out to dinner alone together, ever," I said.

"It's nice."

"Dad, I want to start off by saying I love you and Jillian. And the girls—they are my sisters, my family."

"I'm happy to hear that, Michelle," he said. "But I'm sure there's more you wanted to talk to me about than just that."

"Yes."

"Okay so, spill it." He leaned toward me from across the table.

"I don't want this to come off the wrong way, and the last thing I want to do is fight, so I want you to understand that," I started. "But I've built up a lot of anger over the years, and I need to talk to you about it."

My father was surprisingly receptive, and the conversation remained civil. We spoke quite a bit about everything from the divorce, to his and Jillian's wedding, to how he and my mother treated each other in front of me and Sam. The one thing we didn't talk about was the incident at Oak Beach.

He listened, and then I listened. And as we did, questions arose that neither of us could answer. Should my father have stayed in a loveless, chaotic marriage to support his young children? Or was the answer to move on for his own mental health? After hearing his side of the story, we came to a mutual understanding, one of respect, and even though I didn't agree with him on everything, I forgave him. And when I did that, I essentially forgave myself.

The dinner ended and I gave my father a kiss goodbye knowing he would tell Jillian what we spoke about, and to me, that was okay. I wanted her to understand my side of the story because she never saw it, or if she did, she never truly understood it. I couldn't blame her for that.

Up until this point, Jillian and I had always been cordial with each other, keeping up appearances so we didn't cause unnecessary drama. Following the conversation with my father though, we intrinsically formed a deeper bond, one that was loving and more than superficial. Jillian and I never put it into words, but we both valued the unspoken understanding between us.

~

It was now July 2018, one month after Seth and I married. Mom's Alzheimer's diagnosis was closing in on four long years, and her mental state had declined dramatically. She rarely spoke and when she did, it was almost always unintelligible. Every so often though, for a quick moment, her memory would return, and she'd look at me with a spark of recollection, which would always disappear as quickly as it came.

Mom, Seth, and I sat in a booth at the local burger restaurant we frequented. Seth tried to engage with my mother, but she was hardly cognizant, mostly unaware of her surroundings. There were the rare times though, when she would surprisingly give me a quick smile, almost as if to say, "Michelle, you're doing well."

"Seth and I are adopting littermate puppies!" I exclaimed.

"I would rather live with you, Janet, but I guess I'll have to settle for Michelle and two dogs," Seth quipped.

My mother gave a quick smile. Then, clear as day, and quite unexpected, we heard my mother speak.

"Babies."

It was now I who was speechless. I looked at her in frozen awe as my mother hadn't spoken a coherent word in more than six months, and for a single moment, I felt a glimmer of hope that she was still with us. Then, just as quickly as it happened, she drifted away again.

"One day, Janet. I promise," Seth said, breaking the silence as I continued staring. Though I felt hopeful, I grabbed Seth's hand and held it tight knowing Mom may never meet our children.

Two months later, Seth and I started trying for a baby. Right before the wedding, we purchased a house about fifty minutes south of Nutley. It was a quaint three-bedroom colonial located down the street from a small beach overlooking the Sandy Hook Bay. It had a small backyard, full basement, and the third bedroom was perfect for a nursery. We were excited to bring a child into the life we built for ourselves.

Unfortunately, it was difficult for us to get pregnant.

"Oh sweetie, come here," Seth said, wrapping his arms around my waist in the parking lot after our doctor's appointment.

"I felt it this time, Seth," I said. "I thought it was going to be different."

And I did. After we lost our first pregnancy at seven weeks, and even though I was crushed, we were told that having back-to-back miscarriages was incredibly rare. When I found out I was pregnant again one month later, I was ecstatic. Though we didn't tell many people right away, I spent the next three weeks thinking of baby names, colors for the nursery, and ways we could spread the news to our family. All that planning, that anticipation, that excitement ended abruptly though when the doctor confirmed there was no heartbeat. We were on our second miscarriage in three months.

"Maybe we should try using your frozen eggs like you said," Seth suggested, giving me a kiss. "We will be okay."

After discussing that idea with the doctor, we decided to move forward with the plan and try a round of IVF. We ended up starting the medication three months after our second miscarriage in February 2019, and I had an embryo transfer that April. Ten weeks—sixty-eight straight days—of twice-daily hormone injections and driving an hour each way to the weekly doctor visits back in Hoboken left us with nothing. The transfer had failed.

We had to wait another two months before trying again so my hormone levels could return to normal. Two months sounds like a short time looking back, but when I was living this hell, it felt like an eternity. What added to the suffering was knowing my mother was battling for her mind, and she only had so much time left.

"Should we try another round of IVF, Doctor Hart?" I asked as I sat in the leather chair in front of her desk, holding my husband's hand. Never once did Seth miss a doctor's appointment.

Doctor Hart was a short, full-bodied woman who radiated comfort and reassurance. "We can if you want, but it's another round of medication and hormone injections. If you don't think you're ready, maybe we could try progesterone supplementation," she suggested. "Although it is very rare that this be the cause of your miscarriages, your levels are very low, and I think it could help. What do you think?"

I liked Doctor Hart because she would take our opinion into consideration before making any decision. "Yes, I think we could try that," I said as Seth nodded in agreement. We walked out of the office, and Seth and I smiled at each other with renewed hope.

Unfortunately, that cycle did not result in a pregnancy and I was devastated. "Seth, what are we going to do?" I asked, crying with the negative test still in my hands as he held me tightly.

"I don't know, Michelle," Seth said. "I don't know." He had always looked at life through a positive lens, but this time, he didn't know what to say. I hugged him knowing we'd somehow get through this.

There is really no way to describe the struggle of infertility, and I've only touched on it here briefly since I could probably write an entire book on the topic. For us, it was a never-ending cycle of hope, a possibility of pregnancy that would fill us with excitement, only to turn quickly to heartbreak, always wondering if we'd ever be able to bring a child into this world.

But then, in August 2019, one year after we started trying, I found out I was pregnant with a boy. It was around the sixteen-week mark, and Seth and I had just shared the news with the rest of our family and friends. I was sitting on the deck overlooking our backyard, the large oak tree's leaves changing colors, and our littermates, Peanut and Cookie, at my feet. I looked down at my protruding belly and thought about the type of mother I wanted to be.

I wanted to raise my son to respect women, just like his father. I wanted him to witness a mother and father who got along and were truly happy. I wanted to enjoy Christmas as a family by the fire and birthdays in the yard and sports on weekends and everything else I didn't get to experience as a child.

I wanted him to have the life I never had.

~

Around that time, in December 2019, I made the decision to put Mom into a nursing home. For years, she hadn't been in any shape to be left alone overnight, and after thinking about her safety, I took it upon myself to finally make the decision.

My mother's insurance covered the costs as long as the home was on the list of approved facilities. Unfortunately, many were run-down and filled with staff who seemed mostly hostile and unhappy. I visited over fifteen homes in our area before we came upon Newport Nursing, located thirty minutes from where Seth and I lived. The facility was a bit outdated, but the staff and nurses seemed to care about their patients, and as soon as I walked through the front door, I knew it was the right place.

Newport was divided into three sections based on how much care each patient needed; based on their assessment, my mother needed the most help. She was placed in the dementia unit that housed about thirty others in similar condition. It was bright and airy and though I hated how her life had come to this, I recognized this was the best decision for everyone, including my mother.

The nurses took a liking to her since Sam and I visited often. As a result, Mom was moved into a private room at the end of the long hallway where she could enjoy peace and quiet away from the ruckus of the communal space. I brought her flowers to brighten up the space.

After my mother was settled, I sat next to her on her bed. "Mom, the nurses will take care of you here, I promise," I told her as I rubbed my belly. "Ooh, you want to feel him kick?" I asked. When she didn't respond, I took her hand and placed it underneath mine. When she finally realized what she had just felt, not only did Mom smile, but she also laughed the heartiest laugh I had heard in years. This was the moment she had been waiting for.

Four months later, in April 2020, I gave birth to a son when the world shut down. And as much as I knew my mother wanted to hold that little boy in her arms, I don't think that mattered as much as seeing the joy in her daughter's eyes.

~

Two years passed and it was now April 2022. I was writing in my diary when I received the phone call.

"Hi, Michelle?"

"Yes," I answered.

"This is Mrs. Drummond. I'm sorry to do this but we need you to come to the facility over the next day or two. There is something we'd like to discuss with you," she said. Mrs. Drummond was the director of Newport.

"I can be there tomorrow." I felt a bit of hesitation. "Can you tell me what is going on?"

"I think it's better we do this in person. I will also speak to your sister," she said.

"Okay, thank you."

I smiled when I saw Sam in the parking lot. Although Sam and I were leading two very different lives at the time—me, married with a baby and pregnant with our second; Sam, dating and not ready to settle down—we always connected over our mother. Nothing could destroy what bound us in the first place; she would always be my sister.

"What do you think they want to talk about?" I asked.

"I'm guessing her medication?"

"I hope so," I said, though I knew it was going to be something more than that.

Sam and I walked down the long hallway to Mom's unit. To the right of the communal space, there was a small conference room reserved for conversations between family and the medical staff. The director along with two nurse specialists joined us.

"Thank you for coming," the director said. "The doctor will be here shortly."

"Can you tell us what this is all about?" Sam asked.

"The doctor will explain everything," she said.

Just then, the door opened. The doctor, who I did not recognize and whose name was never given, was short and thin, and wore thick black glasses. She spoke candidly and quickly.

"We believe it is time for your mom to go on hospice," she told us not ten seconds after she sat down in the chair.

"What...what did you say?" I asked, unsure if I heard the words correctly.

"Unfortunately, we feel your mother needs to be in a medical center on hospice care," one of the nurse specialists confirmed. She showed a bit more tenderness.

"What does 'hospice' mean?" Sam asked.

"Hospice requires that we take her off all medication, except for any pain relievers to make her comfortable," the doctor explained.

I looked at Sam, and it was clear we each knew what the other was thinking. I turned my attention back to the doctor. "How long does she have?" I asked.

"We can't know for sure, but usually in these situations, we are looking at a couple weeks to maybe a month," the nameless doctor said.

"No, no that can't be. She's okay. She's not great, but she's okay," I urged.

"Right. She's fine. She can't speak, but that's just the disease," Sam said in agreement.

"Your mom has stopped eating," the nurse said, expecting me and Sam to fully understand what that meant.

"What do you mean she's stopped eating?" I asked confused.

"I'm so sorry, but that usually means it's over," the second nurse added.

"It's over?" I asked, not believing someone could use such words in a situation like this. "You mean, she's going to die. You can just say it."

"Yes, unfortunately," she confirmed. "But we need your consent to move forward."

"I want to see her now."

The doctor opened the door and led me and Sam down the hall to Mom's room.

Mom was lying in her bed under a blanket covered in faces of my son, her face turned toward the window. It was cloudy outside and light rain was tapping on the glass. She looked sickly and frail, her face sunken as if she had lost quite a bit of weight.

"Hey, Mom, I love you," I said as soon as I walked into the bedroom.

"Hi, Mommy," Sam said.

"It's us—Michelle and Sam. We've missed you," I said.

Mom didn't speak. We sat with her for an hour, the room mostly silent. After we left, Sam and I agreed to put her in the end-of-life care unit at the nearest hospital.

~

Every morning at sunrise, before my son woke, I drove forty minutes to Center Hospital and alone, I sat next to my mother. She was even more pale than she looked at Newport and lay motionless under the covers of her hospital bed. She wasn't always asleep though and would stare at me with this oddly beautiful happiness that I was there sitting next to her. I don't know if she knew where she was, or even who I was, but maybe her ignorance made it easier for me to deal with the inevitable. I spent most of my time telling stories about our childhood, and though I recognized I could very well be speaking only to myself, I spoke as if she was fully aware.

Not only did I tell stories, but I also apologized. I apologized for being difficult as a teenager. I apologized for my decision to put her in Linden Hospital eight years ago. I apologized for walking away when she needed me the most, when she was losing her memory. I just kept apologizing for anything and everything I could think of, knowing full well it wasn't going to change a thing.

Over the next week, Mom's breathing grew heavier, and she started gasping, fighting with every breath she took. It was then that her doctor suggested a morphine drip to keep her comfortable. Doctor Grant, who specialized in end-of-life care, was compassionate and caring, and brought a sense of comfort whenever she was near.

Sam and I sat side by side next to our mother when the doctor continued her explanation. "The morphine drip will help with the pain," the doctor explained. "I want to be clear though, your mom will not wake up again once she's on it."

"What do you mean?" Sam asked.

"Your mom will fall into a consistent twilight sleep and then God will take her when she is ready," she said. It was strange for me to hear a medical doctor speak in religious terms.

"I see," I said. "Thank you. We will talk it over and let you know shortly."

The doctor left the room, and it was now just the three of us, just like it had been when we were kids. It felt like it was yesterday that we were back in Nutley living under the same roof in the house on top of the hill.

I looked at Sam. We knew the answer. "I think we need to tell her goodbye, Sam," I said.

"Can I get a few minutes with her alone?" Sam asked.

"Of course."

I quietly walked out of the room and down to the shared bathroom at the other end of the hallway. There, the tears flowed down my face. It was a slow, steady cry, and the pain I felt was excruciating. My agonizing scream could have been heard from down the hall if it were not silent.

I took a deep breath, wiped my eyes and waited in the hall on the bench outside my mother's room. A few minutes later, Sam opened the door, her head in her hands.

I walked into the room with red puffy eyes, and a smile on my face. My mother looked up at me as I spoke.

"Hey, Mom. Do you remember the times we spent hours playing in the yard with Max building obstacle courses, or the times we watched movies on the couch together, or the times we played dress-up in the playroom?" I kept thinking of new memories and hoping, praying that some could reach her. "Remember it all when you go. Remember it all when you think of me and Sam. I love you so much, my Mommy."

I gave her a kiss on her forehead and walked out of the room. Shortly after, the nurse administered the morphine.

~

The week went by with no change in Mom's condition. She never woke up, lying motionless even through the continued visits from family and the hospital noises surrounding her. She just wouldn't let go.

"Mom, what's keeping you?" I whispered close to her ear during one of my morning visits. Then, I paused, suddenly realizing what needed to be done. I took my phone out of my pocket.

"Dad, I'm here with Mom in the hospital," I began, but the knot in my throat made it difficult to speak. I took a breath and continued. "She won't go and I think you need to speak with her. Can you do this for me? Please?" I wasn't sure what to expect with my request.

"Yes, put the phone next to her on the bed."

I stayed in the room as he spoke. It was the first time I had ever heard my father talk to my mother in such a calm, happy way. I was sure he had done so previously at some point in their lives, but it was long before I could remember.

When he was finished, I hung up the phone, took my mother's hand and said, "Mom, it's okay to go now."

And that night, she was gone.

~

My mother's funeral took place on a beautiful Sunday afternoon. I was accompanied by my husband and son and led the motorcade that drove through Nutley past the tudor-style house with brown shutters to the church where I gave my eulogy. Mom in her casket was then taken to the cemetery to be buried in a plot on a hill alongside a tree-lined street.

~

In the days that followed, I made sure to let the grief of my mother's passing sit with me. I allowed myself to feel the pain, to let myself cry, and I didn't search for anything to fill the void. It was the only way for me to process it. Seth also lost a parent when he was in his early thirties, so I had someone to lean on when I had a hard time piecing together what was happening. Because I didn't bury the pain like I had done in the past, I was able to accept that my mother was no longer with me, at least in this world.

Looking back, I remember I felt a lot of guilt over the way I used to argue with my mother and how I hadn't spent as much time with her as I could have. This, I learned, was a big part of the grieving process. Over time though, as I started to think back to the many other times I felt this way, be it blaming myself for every bad thing that happened or making decisions that I second-guessed myself on or the times when I was not perfect, I realized that neither regret nor shame held any purpose in my life. It did nothing to change what happened, and it did nothing to enhance my future. It was just there, consuming my thoughts, adding zero benefit. At every point in my life, there was one thing I could not argue—I had made the best decisions I could at the time. That in itself was all I needed to let the feeling go, because in my heart, I knew I was a good person.

As I learned to release the guilt and shame, I also reflected on how I allowed others to treat me. In years past, I accepted mistreatment because I would let everyone else define my sense of self-worth—Ian, Oliver, Jack, Paul, Drew, and so many others. Now, I realize how damaging and utterly wrong that was.

I learned to not only value myself, but to expect that anyone who came into my life would treat me with trust and respect because no one but myself was in charge of my own happiness. I realized that I, and I alone, was responsible for changing into the person I wanted to become.

~

Some months later, right before Christmas, I sat on the couch, a cup of tea in my hand, a journal on the side table, and my dogs cuddled up next to me. The house was decorated with garland and festive ornaments, and holiday scents filled our home. I looked at my husband, whose laughter echoed through the living room. He sat on the floor next to our two boys, the baby giggling in his swing and my older son, happily building a castle of blocks.

I picked up my pen.

This, I thought, *this is who I was meant to be.*

And I finally felt free.

Note From the Author: Thank you so much for reading! Your support means the world to me. You can help other readers discover this book by leaving a review on Amazon and Goodreads. Every review matters!

About the Author

Since she was a young girl, Michelle enjoyed writing in her diary. However, she didn't seriously consider writing a book until more recently. Prior to her career as an author, Michelle worked in finance for a large corporation, finding it stressful and unfulfilling. It was when she gave birth to her first child in April of 2020 that she decided to focus her energy on her family and raising her son.

During this time, she pursued writing as a hobby and started working on her first comedic feature screenplay. She realized how much she enjoyed the process of artistic creation and continued it through her book. *Stretched* is her first published work and she hopes to continue her love of writing through future novels and screenplays. Michelle is a happily married, stay-at-home mom of two boys.

To see what Michelle Cray is up to, follow her on social media:

Instagram – michellecray

For more stories, visit her website:

www.michellecray.com